Handbook for Deliverance

Phillip Goldfedder, M.D.

HANDBOOK FOR DELIVERANCE

ISBN: 978-0-9824145-7-6

Published by

LIFEBRIDGE
BOOKS
P.O. BOX 49428
CHARLOTTE, NC 28277

www.LifeBridgeBooks.com

Printed in the United States of America.

DEDICATION

This book is dedicated to my wife, Maureen, a woman who treats me like her husband, her brother, her son, her friend, her companion, and her doctor, depending on my given situations and challenges. Her talents as a wife, a gourmet cook, an actress, an artist, a nurse, a mother (of five beagles), a counselor, a speller, a legal advisor, and a case manager have continued to satisfy all my unpredictable needs throughout our years of a blessed marriage. Maureen's fanatical, enthusiastic devotion to me is really beyond my ability to understand or explain.

From a Jewish point of view, I got myself such a good deal. My personal belief is that God orchestrated our godly relationship, that I would grow up and live with a beautiful woman, one who is the ideal help meet for all seasons and for all reasons.

Thank you for your patience, Maureen. I love you. As a reward, I promised her in our next house there won't be a kitchen, just vending machines!

Contents

INTRODUCTION

The purpose of this book is to expose you to the ultimate battle we face—to conquer your enemy, the deceiver, and free the captives from bondage.

Whether you are a minister, counselor, health professional, or a believer who wants to be armed with spiritual power, what you are about to read will give you the authority to act on God's behalf—to bring deliverance to those who are desperately in need.

As a physician, much of what I have to say is directed specifically to doctors. Why? Because I am convinced that when spiritual healing and deliverance is linked with the practice of medicine, there is no limit to the healing that takes place.

This is a spiritual battle, and that is why I want to provide you with signs, wonders, and miracles for handling deliverance. You are being prepared for your ultimate destination—to engage in warfare in a supernatural conflict against the demonic world.

So many churches have been systemically infiltrated by demonic activity in these last days. There is much research which strongly suggests that there are as many Christians who need deliverance, as there are Christians who need healing.

We are in the end-time harvest when both the seeds of good and evil are coming to full fruition. God is calling us to arise and take a strong stand against the works of darkness because we were created for victory.

"And from the days of John the Baptist until the present time, the kingdom of heaven has endured violent assault, and violent men seize it by force [as a precious prize—a share in the heavenly kingdom is sought with most ardent zeal and intense exertion]" (Matthew 11:12).

A SPIRITUAL PHENOMENON

Here is an important synopsis of this critical situation as the late teacher/evangelist Lester Sumrall saw it. He taught that if all the men in the world were doctors, and if all the woman in the world were nurses, and if all the homes were hospitals, we would still have sickness and disease because this is a spiritual phenomenon due to the intense demonic activity that exists on the earth.

The churches are not battling this since they are not able to recognize the need. It comes as a shock to many when they look in a phone book or Internet directory and see the number of witches and warlocks located in their area.

The responsibility I have been given regarding the contents of this *Handbook for Deliverance* is to present what I believe the Lord desires for you to know.

JUST DO IT!

God has already blessed you with your commitment as a physician and He will continue to do so as you enter with Him into His spiritual domain. In this realm, there is no limit or restrictions with time or space. You will learn how vital it is to be free to express what the Father asks you to speak and do. This means regardless of whatever you hear Him say or do, whether or not it makes sense, even if it seems irrelevant, just do it!

It's your obedience that will enable you to free your patients. Your heavenly Father is looking for those who will do and say what He asks, regardless of how foolish it seems because He always has a purpose!

Turn everything over to Jesus and start depending on Him rather than yourself. This means you can depend on Him to give you the desires of your heart. As you listen to Him, continue to become more obedient.

After all, obedience is better than sacrifice. This was made clear when Samuel said, *"Has the Lord as great a delight in burnt offerings and sacrifices as in obeying the voice of the Lord? Behold, to obey is better than sacrifice, and to hearken than the fat of rams"* (1 Samuel 15:22).

Demons are No Match for the Word

When you minister to people, listen and obey the Holy Spirit. You will be surprised how often you will hear from your patients, "How do you know that about me?" or "It's like you're reading my mail," or "Who told you that?"

This is the word of knowledge you are receiving, being told what to say and how to minister for that particular medical situation. Your attitude toward the Word has to be the same as your attitude toward God because this is what's going to make the difference for your success. You can't help but bless your patients as they get healed when they understand their challenges with these demonic spirits are no match for the power of the Word.

The key is that you don't need to fight the devil with experience, but by the written holy Word of God. Your weapon against the devil is Scripture while Satan's success is dependent on your patient's ignorance of the Word.

GOD'S PURPOSE AND PLAN

The truth is that your patient is no longer under the control of the evil one. You have to encourage them to know and believe this for it to be effective. Jesus took away the devil's armor when He removed his primary weapons which were:

1. Accusations.
2. Condemnations.
3. Guilt.

Those you minister to can use these great recommendations for success which will bless them:

1. Depend on the Holy Spirit and be led.
2. Humility.
3. Deliverance from self or ego by submitting to the cross.

Scripture tells us: *"Grace and spiritual blessing be to you and [soul] peace from God the Father and our Lord Jesus Christ (the Messiah), Who gave (yielded) Himself up [to atone] for our sins [and to save and sanctify us], in order to rescue and deliver us from this present wicked age and world order, in accordance with the will and purpose and plan of our God and Father"* (Galatians 1:3-4).

Your Power

The Bible says the devil has no control over believers because of the power from the Holy Spirit that is within us. This makes him accountable to you. Those you are trying to help need to know this. The demons are subject to you and them through His name. He told you to go in His place: *"But to each one is given the manifestation of the [Holy] Spirit [the evidence, the spiritual illumination of the Spirit] for good and profit"* (1 Corinthians 12:7).

Incidentally, when you live a clean life demonic spirits have to obey you. Your spiritual authority and dominion given to you by Jesus Christ of Nazareth will travel within you so that the demonic spirits will experience fear and alarm whenever your presence is anticipated. However, it's true that they do see you as you see yourself.

Manifestations of Deliverance

As you absorb the spiritual information you will find in this handbook, you will be trained and taught. You will read of supernatural experiences through the Holy Spirit including unlimited miracles, signs, and wonders.

You will also have the opportunity to develop in this realm.

The growth you receive in the supernatural is really already programmed into your DNA. Everything you ever needed was already placed in your brain, where God has stored His treasures for you. God will reveal this as you learn how to pull it out from the supernatural into the natural. The truth is that heaven is really here on earth and you just have to learn how to access it.

You can duplicate these manifestations of deliverance by (1) merely increasing your belief level along with your trust in Him and (2) by adjusting your mind-set with the paradigm shift that has already been revealed to you. This will be easy, because the Bible tells you to get the strength you need from Christ. (See Philippians 4:13.)

While you study this *Handbook for Deliverance,* always remember that your major spiritual textbook is the Bible.

ONE

A NEW HOUR

God has ushered in a phenomenal spiritual era with a new movement of His power that is now being witnessed throughout the globe. A hunger for Him is present in many parts of the world, with some Christian services lasting twelve hours at a time.

Many people, however, want to hold onto their own forms of godliness and do without Him—or they even deny His power. When questioned about their opinion of the Church, they explain that they don't like the structure, but prefer what's real. Their new church needs are focused on various forms of entertainment.

We are living in a different kind of hour than ever before. We are on the battlefield of the Lord, whether we realize it or not. This new generation is no longer happy with just "hanging out" in pizza and ice cream parlors; they prefer to meet in groups involved in séances and demonic spiritual encounters. This is a new revolution that consists of people who are being trained to actually harm themselves.

This appears to be the end of what we call the Church Age and the beginning of what is named the Kingdom Age.

The church of tomorrow is going to be radically different from the present-day church. This is the challenge of our day: *"And if it seems evil to you to serve the Lord, choose for yourselves this day whom you will serve, whether the gods which your fathers served on the other side of the River, or the gods of the Amorites, in whose land you dwell; but as for me and my house, we will serve the Lord"* (Joshua 24:15).

As you turn yourself over to the Lord, you will become well-equipped and spiritually well-educated to face demonic spirits. *"Do you not know that your body is the temple (the very sanctuary) of the Holy Spirit Who lives within you, Whom you have received [as a Gift] from God? You are not your own"* (1 Corinthians 6:19).

GOD CALLS IT MURDER

There are millions who need release from their bondage, from the enemy they have been living under, the enemy that has been making them captives. This includes hurting women and their husbands who have allowed their babies to be torn out of their wombs as if Nazi Germany and the Third Reich still exists.

There have been over fifty million babies exterminated thus far. Society calls this "choice," but God calls it murder. Abortion comes from the spirit of murder, which is from the strongman, the spirit of jealousy.

While I was working in the operating room during the summer as a premed in college, I spoke to a former OB-GYN doctor about an unforgettable life-changing event he experienced. He retired into another field, even though he was still in his youth, because, as he was about to perform an abortion to eliminate the life of a baby, he clearly heard the words, "Don't kill me!" several times.

He told me he was never the same after that, and added, "I'll never forget that day!"

When the term "fetus" is used instead of the word "baby," it apparently makes it easier to perform the abortion. Personally, I don't see the difference. However, America has a challenging future as long as our nation continues to sanction the killing of babies.

The crisis is that abortion becomes a practical necessity because sex is considered recreational. How can this ungodly activity be controlled?

IT IS GOD WHO SUFFERS

I believe change is on the way. We are going to see revival throughout the Church and the rain of the glory of God will capture the hearts of the people. With this unity of believers, recovery will come. Revival is *in* you, and the laying on of hands for healing and deliverance is a great start toward a mighty spiritual rebirth.

Let me share something that is vital about God. As soon as you love somebody, you are no longer independent of them; in truth, you become open to any experiences of their hurts, their rejections, their abuses, their emotions, etc.

God loves and, therefore, His love causes Him to experience the same emotions we feel. This is why Jesus suffered for us.

With abortion, it is really God who suffers, as His newborns are destroyed. But instead of being concerned about the Lord, we constantly ask Him to "fix me, heal me, bless me," etc.

Here is Bible proof of what happened as a result of

man's rebellion against the Almighty:

> *The Lord saw that the wickedness of man was great in the earth, and that every imagination and intention of all human thinking was only evil continually. And the Lord regretted that He had made man on the earth, and He was grieved at heart. So the Lord said, I will destroy, blot out, and wipe away mankind, whom I have created from the face of the ground—not only man, [but] the beasts and the creeping things and the birds of the air—for it grieves Me and makes Me regretful that I have made them"* (Genesis 6:5-7).

We can no longer ignore the work of the enemy. Instead, we must confront Satan at every level. This is why you are needed in the battle of all battles—the war against your very soul.

TWO

THE ONLY SOLUTION

I believe that as the final days of our world rapidly approach, there is a desperate and definite need for a spirit of unity to be established so mankind will be able to deal with the overwhelming challenges that threaten our very existence.

Such unity has never been seen in human history, but it is imperative to our survival in these times. By the spirit of unity I do not mean cloning or conformity, because those are conditions we need to oppose and fight against. Even if human cloning could succeed, it would never include the Holy Spirit. The unity to which I refer will require a level of spiritual knowledge and commitment that goes far beyond anything we've ever experienced before. God always honors and blesses unity.

Why is this spirit of agreement so important? It is the only way in which we will be able to confront and find deliverance from the devastating demonic powers that have brought horrendous devastation and oppression to millions of people who are living their lives in daily bondage.

These individuals need to know that there is a way through and a way out of the demonic despair and domination they are under. As believers unite in the power of the Holy Spirit, we will be able to show them the way to complete freedom and deliverance. These are problems that psychiatrists and psychologists are usually unequipped to deal with, because their focus is on the human mind and soul, not the spirit. Since this is a spiritual matter, the Holy Spirit is the only One who has the answers to the problems. His solutions are found in the Bible, and these are profound answers to the dilemmas facing mankind.

One might say, "Well, the Church already uses the Bible, doesn't it?"

Yes, the Church is using the Bible, but is the Church relying on the spiritual power it provides? The Bible tells us, *"For the Word that God speaks is alive and full of power [making it active, operative, energizing, and effective]; it is sharper than any two-edged sword, penetrating to the dividing line of the breath of life (soul) and [the immortal] spirit, and of joints and marrow [of the deepest parts of our nature], exposing and sifting and analyzing and judging the very thoughts and purposes of the heart"* (Hebrews 4:12).

THE POWER OF UNITY

The Church of Jesus Christ has the answers to the challenges that our world and its people face on a daily basis, but all too often there has been a failure to apply these solutions to the human condition. We need godly leadership and counselors who can take us from the problem to the solution. As the writer of the Book of Proverbs states: *"Where no wise guidance is, the people fall, but in the multitude of counselors there is safety"* (Proverbs 11:14).

Note the word "multitude" here; it speaks to the power that comes from unity. Far too many leaders in our churches do not even recognize the demonic activity which is taking place all around us. There are those who do not even believe in the existence of demons! This being the case, how can such a powerless church be successful and victorious in the spiritual warfare that is so desperately needed today?

Often, many leaders who do acknowledge the reality of the demonic realm are fearful about taking the "risk" of getting involved in spiritual warfare. Why? Because they are afraid that such involvement and the potential criticism it might arouse could jeopardize their income, their homes, their careers, and even their churches.

So many are influenced by New Age teachings that result in churches being socially oriented rather than spiritually directed. Instead of seeking to please God, all too many seek to please man. In so doing these leaders are opening themselves up to evil and evil spirits.

TAKING AUTHORITY

Evil enters the picture when men and women do not know and adhere to the Word of God. Jesus founded the Church so it would have a phenomenal spiritual impact upon this planet. Believers are to be the salt of the Earth and the light of the world. (See Matthew 5:13-16.)

However, today it would be accurate to say that the

world has a greater impact on the Church than the Church has on the world. This is a situation we need to change in the spirit of unity.

Our Lord and Savior, Jesus Christ, is still in the business of healing and deliverance. He is the Great Physician, and He has given us the command and dominion to confront and take authority over the spiritual bondage in which so many find themselves. Through the power of the Holy Spirit we are able to set the captives free, and this we must do without fail.

The only true solution to the problems faced by mankind today is found within the Church of Jesus Christ.

Three

An Unexpected Journey

If you have read my book, *The Physician's and Patient's Handbook for Healing,* you know that I am the least likely person to be writing a book on this topic. In case you haven't read it, let me give you a synopsis.

Our family moved quite often when I was growing up. My eighth school was Central High in Philadelphia, an all boys' school. When I reflect back on this, I often wonder what God's purpose was for me in facing all these new environmental changes. Thank God, I never had to experience another seventh-grade challenge of being the only Jew in the school; however, I guess I would still recommend it if you're looking for a way to develop a great sense of humor!

Questions and Answers

I was a few weeks away from starting the eleventh grade when as I entered the stairwell of our rented duplex apartment, I noticed the door to the first-floor apartment was wide open. I took note of a young man who was sitting on the sofa with his feet elevated. He was wearing shorts and pulling a string back and forth that was tied to his big toe.

After I introduced myself, he informed me that he was a third-year medical student studying the muscles of the foot. I learned that his name was Paul, and he quickly became my friend, mentor, and "answer man."

Much later, as I looked back on that relationship and others, I was amazed to see how God had placed the appropriate people in each level and phase of my life. The more answers I received from Paul, to my questions, the greater the level of my hunger became. It's so true that you become who you hang around with, as I learned in those formative years when the direction of my early career began to take shape.

"WHY AM I WATCHING THIS?"

That same year, I became aware of the first great televangelist, Oral Roberts, who was ministering to huge crowds in tent revivals all over the country. The focus of his ministry was on healing and deliverance. Roberts had the courage to step out with his spiritual beliefs in spite of the challenging controversies his activities created everywhere he went.

After school and on weekends I would look for his program on television and sit glued watching—with increased enthusiasm, but without any understanding, as I attempted to figure out what I was seeing and experiencing.

Rev. Roberts would place his hands on the heads of

people, and, as he touched them, they would fall backwards for reasons I did not comprehend. I would stare at the screen, almost mesmerized, and think how dumb it all seemed to be. Then I would ask myself, "Why am I watching this?"

I never really understood its purpose, but it repeatedly captured my attention. There was no way I would have believed that what I was watching was a spiritual thing that involved healing, especially when I had no particular health issues and wasn't aware of anyone else having them. Nonetheless, I was fascinated by what I was seeing.

Later, I learned that 'enthusiasm' means 'God within' and I would use the last four letters of the word enthusIASM as an acronym: **I** **A**m **S**piritually **M**otivated.

AN ENCOURAGER

Also during the eleventh grade, I had to visit my local doctor to complete a health form for school. What a surprise to find I developed an instant friendship with Dr. Arthur, who became my teacher, as well. He was an encourager, like Barnabas in the Bible was, and I began to visit him frequently, not only at his office, but also when he invited me to his home, as if I were a part of his family. That's one of the reasons why I have became an encourager to others as well, just like you will be to your patients.

Soon thereafter, I was privileged to receive a science book that I interpreted as being restricted to doctors. It was entitled, *Man the Unknown* by Alexis Carrel (1873-1944), a Nobel Prize winner and a surgeon. I read how this experimental biologist kept tissue from a chicken's heart alive for thirty-two years among other amazing stories.

Dr. Arthur told me how he handled certain medical situations, and he shared with me medical tips that he had learned in his practice. I never forgot any of them, especially how to respond to the mother who asks, "What you do think about my new baby?" He told me to say with emotion, "Now, that's a baby!" But he really meant it.

In the first week of twelfth grade, we were instructed to spend the coming weekend focusing on the major decision regarding what we wanted to do for our future career.

Representatives from various colleges would be present at the school in the following week to answer our questions.

Central was an elite academic school that was accredited to issue college-level degrees to its students upon graduation. I remember filling in that form, and I wrote the words "Pre-med" in the appropriate space. Later, I realized that the Holy Spirit knows our destiny certainly even before we do. This choice of pre-med was a bit scary to me, for I knew there was no one in my family who was in the field of medicine.

Why had I made this choice? Perhaps my friends Paul and Dr. Arthur had great influence in my life.

"YOU NEED TO DO SOMETHING!"

In my last year of high school, I purchased a book entitled, *William Sharpe, Brain Surgeon.* I learned amazing things from this neurosurgeon's experience, things that again drastically changed the direction of my life.

I learned that this man happened to attend the same high school in Philadelphia that I was attending! This apparent coincidence made me sit up and listen to what he had to say. I decided to attend Albright College, a small school in Reading, Pennsylvania.

In my second year there, my astrophysics major friend spoke to me in the locker room with the dynamics of an actor. He lifted up his voice and said, "You need to do something in your life and become somebody! Why else were you put here on earth?"

I was already majoring in biology and chemistry as a pre-med student, but this thought had became a major impact in my growth and I adopted it as my lifestyle, as I began to play the role of a motivator.

As a follow-up to this, fifty years later, following our class reunion, I was able to locate his telephone number and was stunned to learn that he had become an atheist. He was basically just existing in life for he had lost his dream.

MUSIC OR MEDICINE?

My mother played the violin in the symphony orchestra, and later she became the bookkeeper for one of the great opera companies. With this influence in my life, I also became absorbed with music, and I took violin lessons from the time I was in sixth grade until the beginning of my first year of medical school. I also took lessons briefly from a student at Julliard School of Music, but I quickly realized I couldn't do both.

Eventually, I played in the Reading Philharmonic and Savannah Symphony Orchestras, and at one time I seriously considered music for my career.

My father played the mouth organ, and so I eventually studied the chromatic harmonica, so I could play classics like Bach, Beethoven, and Brahms. (My current desire is to play the three-stringed, triangle shaped balalaika.)

God continued to "drop" people into my life, as I am sure He does in your life. One afternoon, for example, I was walking through the college gym after a class, and the janitor, a part-time minister, approached me. Within ten minutes, he told me about the ineffectiveness of all my books, including the pre-med ones I was carrying around. With simplicity he shared with me the value of Jesus in the lives of people. It was a powerful message, and the truth of it affected me later in life, but I did everything I could at that time to ignore it, since I was already programmed as a Jew.

A Destiny Decision

The more I reflected back on the path of my life, the more I was impressed with what God had been doing all along. Those early experiences were just the beginning preparation for me to move into the field of medicine, but

I believe the desire to do so had been long in place. One day I would fulfill this destiny through God.

Then, in 1984, while at a business convention, I attended a nondenominational worship service, and I said a prayer I really didn't completely understand. However, it was a simple prayer of salvation, and I had been born again.

Soon thereafter I found myself asking the Lord to fill me with the Holy Spirit, especially when I went to bed at night. But I didn't join a church or become what you would call an "active" Christian.

Until 1991, I was oblivious to God, even though I had accepted Jesus into my heart. I never had a reason to acknowledge Him since I was too involved in me, myself, and I. This is affectionately known as the "I" disease.

HOW COULD I BE REJECTED?

How I was able to get into medical school is a miracle in itself. My brilliant mom, who was also Jewish, played a key role.

As a doctor, I'm sure you know what it was like to wait to hear about your approval (or rejection) from your application to medical schools. The crazy, mixed-up emotions that are associated with waiting to hear are sometimes overwhelming. It finally happened. I got an answer after several weeks of waiting. The result was instant depression! The letter read, "Sorry to inform you that…."

You know the rest! How could I be rejected? Going to medical school was my passion. When I told my mom, who had been referring to me as "My son, the doctor," from the time I was seven years old, said, "Good, that was not your first choice!"

That was true, but I would have accepted it anyway. She advised me to write to the school of my choice and inform them that, "I was already accepted to another place, but that I would prefer to go to their medical school."

I was never comfortable thinking that was a God idea, but I realized, thank the Lord, it was a great idea when I finally got accepted by my first choice. Thank God, my parents were able to pay for my tuition (approximately one thousand dollars a year), plus room and board, which was an extraordinary amount of money at that time.

For me, my study time required an average of six hours nightly after school and fifteen hours each weekend. My toughest course in medical school was epidemiology. They had to pass me, however, because I did well in all my other courses!

OFF TO PARRIS ISLAND

In my matching rotating internship application program, I was fortunate enough to obtain the hospital and the elective of my choice, Reading Hospital and neurosurgery. I thought that would be the toughest and most challenging field I could choose, especially after reading that book about the brain surgeon. Of course, my mother was responsible for me going into neurosurgery since she always told me that in life I always had to get "ahead."

She loved my sense of humor; or perhaps she just put up with it!

Since I had to enlist in the military service, I applied to the U.S. Navy and eventually received notice that I was to be stationed at Parris Island in South Carolina as a Navy lieutenant. It was a unique experience, one I would never forget. My time there was an enormous contrast to medical school, internship, and sometimes even medicine itself.

A CAREER DECISION

The Navy corpsmen I worked with were awesome. My first day of indoctrination doing H and P's (history and physicals) to a huge line of Marine privates started off rather poorly. I wasn't able to hear any heart or lung sounds even when I came to the chest of the third recruit. I stopped and realized something was very wrong. I discovered that one of the corpsmen had stuffed the diaphragm of my stethoscope with cotton!

I learned skills I never knew, including how to examine large groups of young men and women (navy Waves) who were healthy, supervising vaccinations that were administered to hundreds, caring for those men who were confined to the brig, treating the recruits, Marines and their families, and gaining skills in playtime activities, such as bowling, photography, pool, swimming, and shooting on the rifle range. Having made a career decision, I needed to apply for a neurosurgical residency program and obtain an interview.

THE EJECTION SEAT

Since I was very familiar with the Philadelphia area, there was a program I wanted to attend there, and I was sure I would be accepted. I took a risk by depending on my faith and only applied to that one program.

The interview was dependent on flying within a 96 hour leave. To hitch a ride on a TIA single engine jet, I had to pass a high-pressure chamber course. This was easy, my next door pilot friend told me, compared to being hurled fifty feet from the ejection seat in case I had to eject during the flight. Sitting in a chamber at 20,000 feet and without oxygen for a short period of time wasn't difficult, but when they shouted, "Pull," I had to respond instantly and pull the overhead lever on that outside metal platform if I expected to fly and get my interview. I still believed my friend until I pulled that lever on command and only moved some ten feet.. .and passed the course.

I was accepted for my neurosurgical residency and scheduled to begin my four-year neurosurgical program following my discharge from the service.

LEARNING ALL OVER AGAIN

During the time of my service obligation, I developed a unique friendship with a high-ranking navy officer, Captain Fred E. Jackson, who was the Chief of Neurosurgery at the Charleston Naval Hospital in South Carolina. During those two years. I visited him frequently and learned an immense amount of practical neurosurgical training information. It was more like an apprenticeship or a short residency program without the blood, even before my residency ever commenced.

This was just another godly coincidence that involved a man who became a hero to me, in the same way that my next-door pilot buddy had become a friend to me. Fred was a gifted teacher who loved people and was always ready to research and train with his ready-to-go movie camera. This is a tribute to him.

My four-year neurosurgical residency was overwhelming, but thoroughly exciting as well, and it was so enormously different from my past training that it was like going back to medical school and learning all over again, with almost entirely different information. I wonder if you can get addicted or rather dependent on the thrill that comes from learning. Perhaps it has to do with our endorphins and the encephalins.

In 1989, my father was diagnosed with a highly malignant tumor, and the tissue biopsy revealed a sarcoma. Unfortunately, the tumor had become metastatic and untreatable. I was already in neurosurgical practice and immediately understood that there was no amount of medical knowledge that would resolve this. He did have excellent oncologists in a top-notch hospital, however.

UNBEARABLE PAIN

Later that same year, I myself was diagnosed with bilateral plantar fascitis associated with spurs. My prognosis was good in that it was not life-threatening, except my colleagues informed me there was no cure or definitive treatment for this condition. I was told I had to learn how to tolerate chronic intractable pain.

My question was, "Where can I enroll in Toleration School? The challenge was that I couldn't take pain medication while working in the operating suite and worse, taking pain medication was against my philosophy anyhow.

My father died in November, 1990. I was with him the night before as he gradually passed away, suffering with unbearable pain in spite of a morphine drip. Unfortunately, he was not open in any way to receive salvation or even to receive prayer.

I made a promise to myself that I would find some way to help these unfortunate victims even though I believed that in spite of all of my training and knowledge that an answer for healing or even any kind of cure was still possible.

You probably won't be surprised to learn that I found a way to treat patients who were suffering with chronic pain when I met a Medtronics representative who came to my office. The specialized program he offered was referred to as neuroaugmentation. He explained that substances naturally produced by the brain, called beta endorphins, act on the periventricular and periacqueductal areas to alleviate pain.

Neuroaugmentation takes advantage of this system by the use of electrical stimulation of deep brain structures and the spinal cord to relieve debilitating chronic pain.

Soon thereafter, I began to treat patients with neurospinal pain implants and later learned how to implant morphine pumps, mostly to alleviate the useless pain associated, for example, with a malignancy.

FIGHTING THE ENEMY

These units were not the answer, however, which explained why only a small percentage of neurosurgeons were involved in this form of pain treatment. I never realized at the time that there was something that could be done about chronic and terminal conditions. It was very fortuitous that I learned how to have access into the supernatural realm through

Jesus as a result of my personal healing and have the opportunity to get even with the devil through Mark 16:18; *"They shall lay hands on the sick, and they shall recover"* (American Standard Version).

The Bible gives advice to never seek revenge or bear a grudge, but I'm referring to those cases in which we are fighting the enemy, who is also the deceiver. You need to understand that one of the many ways the enemy comes to you is through people, but this includes the media as well. *"You shall not take revenge or bear any grudge against the sons of your people, but you shall love your neighbor as yourself. I am the Lord"* (Levicitus 18:19).

The Hope Factor

As a result of this tragic experience with my dad, I realized one of the major reasons for getting involved in a healing ministry was to have a resource that would give people *hope*. This is in contrast to the times when I've had to inform a patient and their family that nothing else can be done.

Do you have any idea what it's like to have hope or not to have hope? The truth is that hope can lead to faith, but hope is not enough, since you can still die with hope. Here's the difference. Hope is in the head, but faith is in heart. Hope is in tomorrow, but faith is in today.

I've had to treat too many patients, who have no hope just like you have. Their medical condition seemed beyond finding a cure. What a blessing it is to be able to give people hope. But thanks to Jesus, it is better to give people Bible hope. Why? Because Bible hope involves significant faith.

UNEXPECTED—UNEXPLAINABLE

In 1991, a salesman came to my office asking me to purchase an advertisement in his local Christian business telephone book. In exchange, I was supposed to expect enough patient referrals to at least cover the costs.

He spotted a book that was on my desk. It was written by Benny Hinn and was entitled, *Good Morning, Holy Spirit*. When he heard me mention I was scheduled for a vacation at Disney World, he insisted that I visit the author and his church in Orlando. I promptly explained that Jewish people don't go to Christian churches, (although I never considered the service at a business convention as a church).

I was unable to explain to him why I read a Christian book, and I never told him about my chronic, intractable pain.

However, once I was at Disney, my curiosity overcame my tradition and I was advised I had to be at the Orlando church by 6:00 A.M. in order to get a seat. Benny Hinn showed a video from a healing service that had been recorded the previous night with Rex Humbard. It was rather "weird" to me, for I saw all the ministers lying on the platform "praying in tongues," as it was later identified to me.

As I watched this unexplainable, almost Disney-like event, something amazing happened almost instantaneously. In just a moment I felt a powerful "heat" come into both my feet and radiate up my legs. Suddenly, all the pain that I had experienced for so long completely disappeared. I didn't know what had happened, and there was no way I could explain it.

After two and a half years the excruciating pain was instantly gone. I immediately leaped up and started jumping up and down. I had not been able to do this since the condition started, and I certainly couldn't have tolerated the pain that would have resulted from that kind of activity. At the same time, I started crying. I couldn't believe the total and instant relief I was experiencing. I was initially embarrassed as I stood there and I cried until I saw many other people who were also standing. I figured they were probably healed as well.

"Is This Real?"

Then I found myself speaking negative confessions! I was saying everything I train people not to say when they are being instructed on how to get healed and stay healed. I asked myself, "Is this real? How long will this last? Will my pain come back?"

This became my radical, mid-life conversion in which God showed up with my spiritual and physical healing.

However, in the meantime, when I was finally informed that Jesus was responsible for my liberation from this bondage, my intellectual response that traveled from my mind into my mouth and tongue was, "I don't think so!" even though I had experienced a supernatural miracle from God. I was told, "There is nothing wrong in being ignorant; you just don't want to stay there."

Obviously, I refused to acknowledge the Hero of this life changing event in my life because of my lack of knowledge and my pride. This was without doubt the same reason I never allowed myself to be "sucked into" that Jesus "stuff" I had heard and occasionally read about.

You see, I already had my life together, especially in my medical practice. I did ignore for that moment what had happened to my father, however.

I came to realize that there is a cycle that occurs in life. It goes something like this: Pride...leads to...

rebellion...leads to...judgment. Pride and rebellion are the first two sins reported in the Bible and this shows you that the devil had no reason to change his tactics against us, since this cycle always works in the life of every uninformed person.

A New Hunger

In my research, many months, many books and tapes later, I began to feel comfortable with my new paradigm. I knew the Holy Spirit was responsible for my intense desire to read and watch more than 500 books and tapes. This new hunger to learn about the supernatural was revelation to me.

Then I started memorizing Scriptures, because they were very inspiring to me. There was one passage in particular that I would repeat often. It's Isaiah 6:8, and it seemed to "pop" into my consciousness and become momentous in my life. This occurred to me whenever the thought came into my mind that I was going to be on a mission to share what I had learned.

Then I would rehearse this verse in my mind: *"Also I heard the voice of the Lord, saying, Whom shall I send? And who will go for Us? Then said I, Here am I; send me."*

My first book, *Healing Is Yours*, took seven years to write. It was motivated by the preceding Scripture, as well as the miracle of my own healing, and the desperate need to offer some kind of "hope" to the sick and dying.

I am so thankful to God for this opportunity to become involved with healing and deliverance. I could have missed life completely by not joining up with God at all; late involvement was far better than no involvement.

FOUR

OVERCOMING DEMONIC FORCES

What an exciting adventure this has been—seeing the lives of men, women, and young people totally transformed by God's power.

Deliverance means to be set free. In this context, this simply means you have the authority and dominion to remove a person from suffering under demonic bondage. Through your God-given power, you can liberate them by whatever means is necessary from the oppression of demonic spirits and bondage including casting them out, expelling them, and driving out the evil spirits which hold them.

Jesus has given you this authority. Before He ascended back to the Father, He stated: *"These signs will accompany those who believe: They will cast out demons in my name"* (Mark 16:17, New Living Translation).

When you analyze the very spelling of the name, devil, you find that the letter "d" could stand for devil, which is Satan; you could subdivide the other half of the word into the word "evil" which means full of evil.

When you look up the word devil you'll find it is

derived from the Greek word *diabolos* which means "accuser" or "slanderer." In the general midstream of Christianity, the fight between God and the devil is over the "souls" of people in order to keep them from going to hell.

The devil commands a force of demons or evil spirits that you might think came to test humankind, but their intent is to take health and healing from you and everyone else while they themselves are waiting without any option of avoiding the eternal pit.

"THE DEVIL MADE ME DO IT!"

In our secular world there are many misrepresentations and even humor regarding demonic activity perhaps to reduce the fear associated with it. This includes one comedian who became famous claiming, "The devil made me do it."

The challenges are that when people are imbedded with witchcraft, they can't respond to prayer—or for that matter, even medical treatment.

I pray you will feel the compassion of what Jesus did for you: *"Since, therefore, [these His] children share in flesh and blood [in the physical nature of human beings], He [Himself] in a similar manner partook of the same [nature], that by [going through] death He might bring to nought and make of no effect him who had the power of death—that is, the devil"* (Hebrews 2:14).

My Jewish tradition limited my understanding of demonic activity. How could I expect to believe any of this having been exposed only to the left side of the Bible?

BREAKING THE CHAINS

In my youthful years, I viewed the word evil as "live" spelled backwards. Yet, God is quite clear about not allowing yourself to be ignorant or suffering from lack of knowledge. (See Hosea 4:6.)

The absence of knowledge poses great risks to you because the devil's success is dependent upon your ignorance. However, the Word of God destroys the power of the destroyer: *"[But] he who commits sin [who practices evildoing] is of the devil [takes his character from the evil one], for the devil has sinned (violated the divine law) from the beginning. The reason the Son of God was made manifest (visible) was to undo (destroy, loosen, and dissolve) the works the devil [has done]"* (1 John 3:8).

The truth is that these people are not bound by accident or coincidence; they actually make their own choice to join forces with the demonic realm. They don't want to release the devil since he can give them their needed importance in life.

In these cases, deliverance is unlikely to happen for them because they're comfortable right where they are. *"Do you not know that if you continually surrender yourselves to anyone to do his will, you are the slaves of him whom you obey, whether that be to sin, which leads to death, or to obedience which leads to righteousness (right doing and right standing with God)?"* (Romans 6:16).

They make a willful choice to sin and are responsible

for inviting the evil spirits in. The Bible tells us that man shall be held by the cords of his own sins: *"His own iniquities shall ensnare the wicked man, and he shall be held with the cords of his sin"* (Proverbs 5:22).

This lack of instruction is, of course, responsible for people who go astray without God's Word, which allows evil to take control.

Instruction is the key to deliverance: *"They promise them liberty, when they themselves are the slaves of depravity and defilement—for by whatever anyone is made inferior or worse or is overcome, to that [person or thing] he is enslaved"* (2 Peter 2:19).

God's Son spoke to His disciples and told them He received all His authority for both heaven and earth. *"Jesus approached and, breaking the silence, said to them, All authority (all power of rule) in heaven and on earth has been given to Me"* (Matthew 28:18).

WHAT IS THIS?

The Jewish religious leaders marveled with the power and authority Jesus demonstrated over demons since the spirits left merely without a word, even the unclean spirits. *"And they were all so amazed and almost terrified that they kept questioning and demanding one of another, saying, What is this? What new (fresh) teaching! With authority He gives orders even to the unclean spirits and they obey Him!"* (Mark 1:27).

Jesus demonstrated that many demon-possessed men and women were brought to Him and He commanded the demons to leave. He cast out spirits with just a word and the gospels revealed He healed all the sick. *"Now at the setting of the sun [indicating the end of the Sabbath], all those who had any [who were] sick with various diseases brought them to Him, and He laid His hands upon every one of them and cured them. And demons even came out of many people, screaming and crying out, You are the Son of God! But He rebuked them and would not permit them to speak, because they knew that He was the Christ (the Messiah)"* (Luke 4:40-41).

Jesus was also a great instructor teaching His twelve disciples and then appointing an additional seventy-two. *"And Jesus summoned to Him His twelve disciples and gave them power and authority over unclean spirits, to drive them out, and to cure all kinds of disease and all kinds of weakness and infirmity"* (Matthew 10:1). *"And they drove out many unclean spirits and anointed with oil many who were sick and cured them"* (Mark 6:13).

"DEMONIZED"

As Christ-followers we have been given the spiritual power of attorney and authority to bind principalities, powers, and rulers through Jesus. (See Luke 10:19.)

When a person is under the power or influence of a demon or when it is said they have a demon it means they are "demonized."

These demonic spirits have assignments over individuals, homes, singleness, health, finances, etc.

When we bring the Kingdom of Heaven on the scene, we cast out demons and they have to retreat because you are the Kingdom of God. But it's really the Holy Spirit who has the power to cast out devils; we are just tools in

His hands. He shows this in Matthew 12:28: *"But if it is by the Spirit of God that I drive out the demons, then the kingdom of God has come upon you [before you expected it]."*

ESCAPING THE SNARE

Recovery occurs when men and women discover the truth by yielding willfully and knowingly so they can bring themselves out of bondage—just by acknowledging the truth of the Word of God. As Scripture declares: *"He must correct his opponents with courtesy and gentleness, in the hope that God may grant that they will repent and come to know the Truth [that they will perceive and recognize and become accurately acquainted with and acknowledge it], And that they may come to their senses [and] escape out of the snare of the devil, having been held captive by him, [henceforth] to do His [God's] will"* (2 Timothy 2:25-26).

Here's further proof of the importance of being obedient to Him and to avoid traveling the wrong path: *"Whoever observes the [king's] command will experience no harm, and a wise man's mind will know both when and what to do"* (Ecclesiastes 8:5). We also learn, *"He is dressed in a robe dyed by dipping in blood, and the title by which He is called is The Word of God"* (Revelation 19:13).

And the psalmist writes: *"O Lord my God, if I have done this, if there is wrong in my hands, If I have paid back with evil him who was at peace with me or without cause have robbed him who was my enemy, Let the enemy pursue my life and take it; yes, let him trample my life to the ground and lay my honor in the dust. Selah [pause, and calmly think of that]!"* (Psalm 7:3-5*)*.

SUPERNATURAL COMMUNICATION

Again, let me speak directly to physicians. I believe that doctor-supervised deliverance will bring about a much-needed revival that will release glory and peace and free the captives. Your increased opportunities for patient healing and deliverance will reach the same levels of skills and talents you developed as a medical doctor—and more. Your communication with your patients through the supernatural will grow amazingly as it is guided and led by the Holy Spirit. He has appointed you as Head of your Division and permanent Chief of the Service under His direction. You are going to perform what many ministers in churches are unable to do.

Unfortunately, spiritual deliverance is rarely taught in seminaries or in the curriculum of Christian schools of education. There is denial about the existence of demonic spirits which is based on fear that occurs from disbelief —which gives rise to disobedience. Just as in your medical practice, your strength and confidence in taking charge will grow with your experience.

There will be challenges with your patients that will be evident on both sides as you question them about this sensitive and embarrassing situation of evil spirits. Learn how to obtain adequate and sufficient information without being offensive and without compromise to your patient. You need to be able to cast out demonic spirits, their fears, their rejections, their hurts, and heal their wounded memories.

DEALING WITH THE DEVIL

Lucifer, one of the three archangels, rebelled against God and attempted to take his place in heaven because of his pride. This fallen angel contrived to make his throne higher than the clouds and God. His punishment was to be thrown out of heaven along with one third of the angels who rebelled along with him. The remaining two-thirds of the angelic hosts still serve as arms of God.

Satan, the CEO whom you are dealing with, is real, yet has no legal right to harm you since you are a born again, Bible-reading, spirit-filled, Word-speaking believer. You have to discern that the devil knows you better than your mom!

He's good at stealing the Word from you and your patient so consider this as a warning to protect what you hear since the Word can set you free. The devil is intent on keeping you out of the Scriptures.

"I don't understand it," a woman told me, "It looks like the devil is after you guys all the time. He doesn't ever bother me."

"Well," I replied, "apparently you must not be a threat to him."

SATAN'S LIMITS

Scripture describes how Lucifer, who became Satan (this means God's enemy), fell from heaven: *"How have you fallen from heaven, O light-bringer and daystar, son of the morning! How you have been cut down to the ground, you who weakened and laid low the nations [O blasphemous, satanic king of Babylon!]"* (Isaiah 14:12).

What I am about to say is important. Do not fall into the habit of casting Satan out rather than the demonic spirits, for you need to realize that he is not omnipotent. This means, unlike God, he can only be in one place at one time.

An evangelist heard from the Holy Spirit as she stepped onto the lawn of the White House in Washington, D. C., that she would be dealing with Satan who was already there. When she asked why, she heard that he preferred to spend his time where there was political power and authority. There is no power behind your word toward him if you believe he is wherever you are.

YOU CAN BIND SATAN

When you refer to Satan, the devil, you are more likely talking about the minions, evil spirits, demons, or the demonic spirits. Avoid poking fun at him or calling him made-up names; just maintain his name as given even by using a capital S. Otherwise you lose your ability to hurt him with your godly words.

You are supposed to recognize him, the devil, according to the Bible, just as if you were honoring a general because of his authority, not because of the evil in him. You also need to know that you can bind Satan, but you can't rebuke him. Satan comes against your mind because that is where you make your choices. He can become as big in your mind as you allow him because this is the doorway through which he can gain access and fill you with his evil thoughts.

Your goal is to keep Satan from your thought life because he wants to separate you from your faith and what you believe. When you detect ungodly thoughts, just talk to them and tell them to stop in the name of Jesus and command them to leave.

You are in charge and you can refuse to accept negative thoughts. You have to realize who you are dealing with regarding the activities of the deceiver. As the Bible states, *"You are of your father, the devil, and it is your will to practice the lusts and gratify the desires [which are characteristic] of your father. He was a murderer from the beginning and does not stand in the truth, because there is no truth in him. When he speaks a falsehood, he speaks what is natural to him, for he is a liar [himself] and the father of lies and of all that is false"* (John 8:44).

The greatest battle you will ever encounter against the devil is that of guilt and righteousness. He will set you up with guilt so that you begin to believe that you have to fight it on a constant persistent basis even though Jesus totally took it from you when He was nailed to the cross for your sins. This challenge is rather prevalent in the church because the devil's activities persist as exemplified with many sin-centered hymns sung in churches which attempt to keep us aware of this.

THE ONGOING CONFLICT

In your "other" battle, with righteousness, the devil will set you up in an attempt to put you under the law. The truth is that only sin places you under the law, for this is the law of sin and death.

The apostle Paul explained this rather well in Romans 7, which is really based on science. It follows a principle because it reacts the same way every time, everywhere, regardless of the circumstances. It's no different than the way the law of gravity works that was discovered by Newton.

Every time Paul willed to do good, he sinned instead. This continued to happen repeatedly until he discovered he was not rebelling against evil or himself, but something inside him. Even though he wanted to do good, he realized this reaction of evil took place whenever he exerted his flesh or his self-effort to do good.

This alien element, his flesh, was rising up within him to always make him do evil. He knew that attempting to keep the law always caused this evil to occur because of his flesh. The answer is to turn everything over to God and the Holy Spirit rather than your flesh.

Your carnality is a rebel living with you every day, going to bed, waking up, showering. It is your number one enemy and you can't teach or educate him. You have to *execute* him—not just when you become born again, but when you follow Jesus and start living in the Spirit so you can walk in the Spirit.

Destroying the Flesh

The flesh is probably the greatest challenge for those you are trying to help. The reason is that your patient is feeding the flesh by watching the world.

Since the flesh is so strong, the only way to kill it is

by the Holy Spirit. He can help you for He is the only one who will help your patient if they really want Him to. All they have to do is to surrender the flesh on the cross so the Holy Spirit can destroy it. From that point forward, help the person so the flesh will not be resurrected.

Witchcraft is really your carnal flesh, but you have been freed from battling this in the realm of your mind. How? Because it's no longer carnal, but spiritual. John 17:2 confirms this: *"[Just as] You have granted Him power and authority over all flesh (all humankind), [now glorify Him] so that He may give eternal life to all whom You have given Him."*

You must believe that you are under the law of the Spirit of life. Since the Holy Spirit has dominion over you, which He does, you are not under the former law. God's laws provide you with peace, but man's laws will not.

Righteousness comes from belief, faith, and the shed blood of Jesus. You will appreciate this, for when you are established in righteousness, without oppression or fear, then peace will come upon you: "*You shall establish yourself in righteousness (rightness, in conformity with God's will and order): you shall be far from even the thought of oppression or destruction, for you shall not fear, and from terror, for it shall not come near you"* (Isaiah 54:14).

"LORD OF FLIES"

Satan is sometimes referred to as the "Lord of Flies."

It's true that the demonic world is very much like the insect world.

Did you ever consider all the death and destruction that is brought on by insects which most people essentially ignore? There are an estimated one million different known species of insects on our planet, and some experts believe there are as many as ten million species.

Countless diseases are spread by insects because of organisms that are passed on when they feed or bite. For example, malaria is still one of the leading causes of death and disease in many developing countries even though great gains have been made to control its initial destruction.

Not only can demonic activity affect us by the negativity of the insect world through destruction, but also by destruction of the *positivity* of the insect world of bees.

THE ANTIDOTE FOR EVIL

Bees are an engineering marvel from their aerodynamics, to their shell, to their sensors, and especially for their ability to pollinate. They are responsible for pollinating thirty percent of the nation's food supply which amounts to over 20 billion dollars a year in seeds and crops.

However, in recent years there has been a significant tragedy occurring that is affecting bees called Colony Collapse Disorder. What has been happening is that mature bees are abandoning their hives and disappearing followed shortly thereafter by their queens and young ones. There is great concern about the potential of famines because of the food shortages that have already been reported. Wild pollinators such as native bees, wasps, and butterflies are also suspected to be in sharp decline.

In this same way, Satan, the Lord of Flies, will do everything in his power to spread death and destruction.

Thankfully, we know the antidote for his evil schemes. We have the power of God's Spirit, which is greater than he who is in the world.

FIVE

THE DEMONIC REALMS

Satan never comes to us as the devil, but always as an angel of light. As you would guess, his first temptation appears as an opportunity for good, but he functions through deception.

Here are eight ways Satan manifests his power:

1. Through temptation to sin.
2. Through accusation in multiple ways: before God, against God; before the brethren, against the brethren; to God against the brethren; to the brethren against God.
3. Through opposition to the work of God.
4. Through confusion to truth.
5. Through idolatry and magic.
6. Through many antichrists.
7. Through structural or organized evils.
8. Through demons.

YOUR ADVERSARIES

Demons are disembodied spirits on earth that are

always hunting for a body so they can manifest their wickedness in the natural world and continue their evil ways. They would even prefer an animal body to dwell in rather than do without one or even live in an inanimate object. Otherwise, they go into torment when they don't have a body to inhabit.

Since they are without corporate bodies, they can go through solids (like walls). These are invisible beings and can't be seen because they exist on the molecular level.

The demonic realm attempts to sneak past people's awareness by exaggerating their activities in horror and vampire movies. As a result, the world takes demons as a joke, but they are absolutely real.

The devil wants you to believe they don't exist by being ridiculous on the one hand and subtle on the other. The bottom line is that you and the church are the only authorities able to oppose him.

THE ROARING LION

The enemy you are fighting is a highly organized military machine carefully trained to never break rank. They do employ a supernatural power, but it's counterfeit. These demons exist in the air above us in the second heaven which is their abode and where they carry out the base of their operations. But we are in the first heaven and have authority over them, while God and the angels are in the third heaven—who of course exist without the need for a body.

Just to give you an idea of what you are getting involved with, you might be surprised to learn that there is a name of a demon for every conceivable emotion or condition that people have, and some you or I have never heard about as yet.

When people demonstrate emotions such as temper, anger, depression, fear, resentment, bitterness, anxiety, etc., they can develop demonic activity as the result of their pressing into their emotions. We give the demons the legal right to enter our body and mind because of our persistent behavior.

The devil appears as a roaring lion and makes plenty of noise, but he really isn't, even though he certainly acts as if he were. We are told: *"Be well balanced (temperate, sober of mind), be vigilant and cautious at all times; for that enemy of yours, the devil, roams around like a lion roaring [in fierce hunger], seeking someone to seize upon and devour"* (1 Peter 5:8).

FIVE DEMONIC REALMS

God's Word tells us exactly what we are up against. *"For we are not wrestling with flesh and blood [contending only with physical opponents], but against the despotisms, against the powers, against [the master spirits who are] the world rulers of this present darkness, against the spirit forces of wickedness in the heavenly (supernatural) sphere"* (Ephesians 6:12).

These spiritual entities involve dark powers which seek to influence your mind, your will, your senses, and your emotions against God. We are actually wrestling against the following five divisions of spiritual demonic realms rather than against physical weapons:

One: Demons or hosts are the vast multitudes of foot-soldiers in Satan's kingdom.

They are in the atmosphere and in people. Ephesians 2:2 tells us how they work in the sons of disobedience. *"In which at one time you walked [habitually]. You were following the course and fashion of this world [were under the sway of the tendency of this present age], following the prince of the power of the air. [You were obedient to and under the control of] the [demon] spirit that still constantly works in the sons of disobedience [the careless, the rebellious, and the unbelieving, who go against the purposes of God]."*

Two: Principalities are the chief rulers and strong spirits of the highest powers that seek to exercise dominion over particular geographical zones.

Three: Powers are stronger spirits and authorities that influence respective cultures in certain negative ways.

For example, there are significant religious traditions in some cultures that are working to blind the eyes of people to the gospel as revealed in 2 Corinthians 4:4: *"For the god of this world has blinded the unbelievers' minds [that they should not discern the truth], preventing them from seeing the illuminating light of the Gospel of the glory of Christ (the Messiah), Who is the Image and Likeness of God."*

There are also cultures with strife, lust, idolatry, or even witchcraft operating to varying degrees.

Four: The world rulers of the darkness of this world are princes and wicked men in the spiritual realm throughout all the nations of this world. Satan is the prince of the power of the air.

Five: Spiritual wickedness in high places are wicked spirits and fallen angels who have infiltrated the religious systems of the world including the congregations of the righteous.

SATAN'S COUNTERFEIT

When you deal with individuals who are nonbelievers and who believe in reincarnation, there is an urgent and serious need for them to be released from demonic involvement because this is not biblical and consequently considered a spirit of antichrist. The Bible declares, *"And just as it is appointed for [all] men once to die, and after that the [certain] judgment"* (Hebrews 9:27).

Satan has counterfeited God's army which also consists of five divisions including the 1) seraphim, 2) cherubim, 3) living creatures, 4) archangels, and 5) angels.

The seraphim introduce and present the glory of God.

CLUES REPRESENTING DEMONIC ACTIVITY

Those who deal with casting out demons report several subtle clues to their activity. Some may seem like natural responses or innocent appearing activities, but when combined with other signals you can discern a satanic presence. These clues include:

1. Coughing.
2. Yawning.
3. Belching.
4. Sneezing.
5. Vomiting.
6. Eye blinking. Their eyes can reveal ongoing demonic activity.
7. Foul odors such as sulphur.
8. Pain that moves in the body.
9. Manifestations of talking.

When a manifestation occurs, that is, when the demons begin to talk through the person, you can often hear a different voice even one of the opposite gender.

Jesus wouldn't allow manifestations to occur because demons never speak the truth—nor can they be trusted as to what they say. He never got involved tolerating this except with the Gadarene demoniac (Mark 5).

DEMONIC ACTIONS AND ACTIVITIES

According to Scripture, demons can apparently perform the following:

1. Demons seek and search.
2. Demons have emotions and need rest.
3. Demons have intelligence.
4. Demons have eyes because they can see.
5. Demons can talk.
6. Demons have a will and can make decisions and can plan.
7. Demons have faith.
8. Demons have memory.
9. Demons have personalities.
10. Demons can think which affords them an imagination.
11. Demons can recruit one another during offensive activities.

How They Come In

Demons enter an individual because sin gives them the legal right to do so.

The Bible clearly records one such event because of sin that occurred with Judas Iscariot who was one of the twelve disciples: *"Then after [he had taken] the bit of food, Satan entered into and took possession of [Judas]. Jesus said to him, What you are going to do, do more swiftly than you seem to intend And make quick work of it"* (John 13:27).

Here are 26 reasons demons enter an individual:

1. Lack of the Word.
2. Unforgiveness.
3. The carnal mind.
4. Profane use of inappropriate words (swearing).

5. Yielding to sin.
6. Involvement with the occult.
7. Rebellion.
8. Slander.
9. Laziness or slothfulness.
10. Void of understanding.
11. The wrong confession.
12. Hereditary and generational curses through bloodlines.
13. Inviting themselves by their own choice.
14. Victimization from trauma or weaknesses that develop.
15. Sins of commission through their legal spiritual rights.
16. Sudden shocks, traumas, loud noises, and crises.
17. Rituals of non-biblical religions and secret societies.
18. Hurts and wounds from others.
19. Covenants, religious festivals, and pilgrimages.
20. Idolatry, cursed objects, occultic sins.
21. Spiritual transfer through grief, terminal illness, ungodly soul ties, and death.
22. Environmental transfer in institutions such as prisons, hospitals, mental and psychiatric asylums usually involving pain and suffering.
23. Sexual transfer involving person-to-person contact with resulting demonic spiritual union.
24. Innocent children sexually abused with lustful spirits.
25. Spirits of resentment, rejection, anger, hatred, and bitterness.

26. Pornography, occultic role-playing games, and devices to communicate with the dead.

GUARD YOUR GATES!

Since demons can enter your life through any door that is left open, we need to be constantly on watch. They can enter through 1) the family gate, 2) the sin gate, 3) the trauma gate, 4) the undisciplined life gate, 5) the religious gate, 6) the relationship gate, 7) the occult gate, and 8) the passivity gate.

SIX

WARNINGS OF WITCHCRAFT

Perhaps the least understood or recognized of the major enemies of God and His people is witchcraft. It can attack the church by releasing its power just like an invading army conquers a city. The general describes his anticipated victory by explaining that his troops come from the north, the south, the east, and the west but his triumph is from the fifth column. That's the presence of his troops inside the city.

Witchcraft is successful because it is the fifth column within the church. The Bible condemns the practice as an abomination. It is the single most damaging threat against the church because witchcraft is the front for legalism and carnality.

Legalism is a subtle religious spirit that attempts to achieve righteousness with God by observing or adding any set of rules. Carnality is allowing your flesh to run the show—which is what witchcraft is. In other words, witchcraft flourishes in the soulish realm which involves three main operations:

1. Spells and curses
2. Divination
3. Sorcery

The ultimate object of all witchcraft, which is the "power arm," is to bring an individual under a curse or a spell.

UNDER A CURSE

Many Christians are under a curse because they have turned away from the Lord and prefer to do things by their own human efforts and therefore depend on their own human power. *"This is the word of the Lord: Thus says the Lord: Cursed [with great evil] is the strong man who trusts in and relies on frail man, making weak [human] flesh his arm, and whose mind and heart turn aside from the Lord"* (Jeremiah 17:5).

Witchcraft brings an individual under a curse because it causes them to disobey God even though they know they can't be touched when they're under God's divine order.

DIVINATION

Divination is the "predictive arm" that operates through fortune telling, crystal balls, tea leaves, and can even predict Satan's destiny on you. For some reason, many people have an overwhelming desire to know what's going to happen in their future which is really contradictory to the Bible.

This desire will allow the devil to obtain a certain control over their life. The demons have a supernatural insight through their demonic power but not people's thoughts—although they readily understand nonverbal communication. Be aware that the prophecy they receive from this kind of demonic activity may very well, unfortunately, come to pass.

SORCERY

Sorcery operates through things such as amulets or charms, potions, and talismans to gain control of people.

You are encouraged to believe that these objects are placed on your body to "protect you." When you translate the Hebrew word *kashaph* which is sorcerer, it means someone who uses magic to harm others.

Sorcery also involves drugs and music. The truth is that the whole drug culture is a form of sorcery including music.

I was on a cruise ship where such music was blasting over the loud speakers. I realized I had to leave the deck because of the rhythm of satanic music. I could see the staring dreamy state of the eyes of teenagers exposed to this type of entertainment.

Rebellion means opposition to one in authority and it involves self deception, control, lawlessness, and witchcraft.

Here is another way to express these activities that are bound together: lawlessness = control = witchcraft = rebellion.

The Bible states in 1 Samuel 15:23, when Samuel

was talking to King Saul: *"For rebellion is as the sin of witchcraft, and stubbornness is as idolatry and teraphim (household good luck images). Because you have rejected the word of the Lord, He also has rejected you from being king."*

The stubborn person makes idols out of his own opinion. The truth is that rebellion and witchcraft are twins—because they seldom exist alone. Did you realize that rejection breeds rebellion? It is also believed that rejection is the root of most demonic strongholds.

DOMINATION, INTIMIDATION, AND MANIPULATION

Witchcraft is a work of the flesh for it comes out of our fleshly nature and it shows up as Domination, Intimidation, and Manipulation. An acronym to remember this is to realize that the devil takes a D.I.M. view of us. One of the favorite tactics of witchcraft is for the person involved to make you feel guilty.

Millions of women operate with D.I.M. because these are the same controls they've learned to use from their mothers and their grandmothers. Authorities on the topic report that ninety percent of witches are women. They don't know any other way because they never appreciated that this became a major part of their personality. Consequently, they can't break from their witchcraft which is one of the reasons they are unable to understand the Bible because it takes the place of the Holy Spirit.

Healing and deliverance requires that they repent

first, followed by a one hundred percent renunciation.

Women are more sensitive than men and the devil takes advantage of this. He rides on their sensitivities. One minister spoke about how he had a dream of a group of Christians running and he saw the devil riding on their backs. The devil is always on their back in witchcraft and people don't realize or know about it. He's so subtle. Even Eve had this experience.

Our three main needs in life are love, security, and significance. When we don't know how to obtain these from God, we resort to witchcraft.

RESULTS OF WITCHCRAFT

Ministers, especially those who are married, need to understand that as the pastor they must make decisions because of their responsibilities to their sheep. Since it's God who speaks to them, they need to yield to His Spirit. Unfortunately, there are few men strong enough to deal with witchcraft in women and consequently, it should be pointed out that there are millions of men who are under witchcraft. It could well be the number one housebreaker that's responsible for divorce in this country.

Witchcraft can develop in them because of the rebellion it produces. It can keep men from maturing both spiritually and emotionally. That is, it inhibits men from becoming successful in the Lord and in their homes, but not necessarily in their businesses.

The witchcraft label is applied when it influences another person's mind, body, or property against his or her will. This has been clearly demonstrated in many cultures that can even be traced back to ancient texts such as those from Egypt and Babylonia. It has become a credible cause for sickness and disease, including animals. It could explain what people refer to as "bad luck," sudden death, impotence, and other such misfortunes.

Regardless of the apparently reported more benign and socially acceptable varieties, there is always great risk to any involvement when you open up your heart or mind to witchcraft.

Witchcraft doesn't have to be demonic, but often turns into it.

SEVEN

STRONGMEN AND SPIRITS

Demons operate in groups, each having a ruler or controller in charge of them. These demon rulers are referred to as strongmen because they run the show and appear depending on whatever conditions or situations occur in your patient. This means if you want to deliver a person, you first need to cast out the strongman rather than the demonic spirit that identifies the person.

Depend on the Holy Spirit for help. For example, if the individual you are working with has an addiction to drugs, the strongman that needs to be cast out is the spirit of bondage and not the spirit of addiction. This same strongman also includes addiction spirits to alcohol, smoking, gambling, etc.

Another example is the strongman spirit of deaf and dumb which must be cast out rather than the spirit of suicide. The spirit of suicide just identifies the person's challenge, but this spirit is not in charge.

These are the strongmen along with their associated spirits:

1. ***The Spirit of Jealousy*** (Numbers 5:11-14)
   • Spirit of Anger • Spirit of Competition • Spirit of Murder • Spirit of Rage • Spirit of Revenge
   • Spirit of Suspicion

2. ***The Spirit of Lying*** (2 Chronicles 18:22)
   • Spirit of Divination • Spirit of Evil Doings
   • Spirit of Hypocrisy • Spirit of Profanity
   • Religious Spirit • Spirit of Superstition • Spirit of Vanity

3. ***Familiar Spirit*** (1 Samuel 28:7)
   • Astrology • Fortune Telling • Horoscope • Occult

4. ***Perverse Spirit*** (Isaiah 19:14)
   • Filth • Fornication • Hating God • Homosexuality
   • Always Twisting the Word of God • Laziness
   • Living in Error • Lust • Men who Lust after Women

5. ***Spirit of Heaviness*** (Isaiah 61.3)
   • Depression • Despair • Gloominess • Gluttony
   • Grief • Hopelessness • Loneliness • Self-pity
   • Self-rejection • Weight Problems

6. ***Spirit of Whoredom*** (Hosea 4:12)
   • Adultery • Always ending up in Poverty • Filthy Spirit • Idolatry • Never Satisfied • No Will of their Own • Perversion • Prostitution • Religious Spirit • Spirit of Error • Idol Worship

*7. **Spirit of Infirmity*** (Luke 13:11)
- All Sicknesses and Diseases

*8. **Spirit of Deaf and Dumb*** (Mark 9:17)
- Anorexia • Insanity • Lunatics • Seizures
- Suicide

*9. **Spirit of Fear*** (2 Timothy 1:7)
- All Phobias • Doubt • Fear of Dark • Fear of Heights • Feels Inadequate • Inferiority Complex
- Nightmares • Sense of Dangers • Terror
- Timidity • Torment • Uncontrollable Tremblings (physical) • Worry

*10. **Spirit of Pride/Haughtiness*** (Proverbs16:18)
- Anger • Brag about Themselves • Contention and Wars Among People • Controlling • Fightings
- Gossip • Mockery • Religious • Self-righteousness
- Stubbornness • Wrath

*11. **Spirit of Bondage*** (Romans 8:15)
- Addiction • Alcoholism • Anguish • Bitterness
- Fear • Spiritual Blindness

*12. **Spirit of Antichrist*** (1 John 4:3)
- Deny the Cross of Jesus • Deny the Deity of Jesus
- Religious Spirit • Deny Resurrection • Deny the Virgin Birth

EIGHT

DEALING WITH SPECIFIC SPIRITS

Many of the strongmen and spirits mentioned in the previous chapter are self-explanatory, but there are several areas in which you need to be aware. They include:

Spirit of Heaviness

One of the ways the spirit of heaviness manifests itself in the church is demonstrated when the people become drowsy and sleepy during the sermons. Command the spirit of heaviness to leave, for the Bible tells us we are to put on *a garment of praise for the spirit of heaviness* (Isaiah 61:3).

Spirit of Infirmity

When you speak about an infirmity, you are referring to a physical weakness or a defect (according to Webster's New World Dictionary).

One of the strongmen listed is called a spirit of infirmity and is a major spirit because it is responsible for almost all of the sicknesses and diseases that exist. This spirit can affect the body as well as the mind, since the mind can become "feeble, weak, and frail."

To cure sicknesses and disease you must cast out this spirit. For example, Jesus commanded the spirit of infirmity to come out of a woman's spine: *"And there was a woman there who for eighteen years had had an infirmity caused by a spirit (a demon of sickness). She was bent completely forward and utterly unable to straighten herself up or to look upward"* (Luke 13:11).

The Bible records that Jesus was anointed with the Holy Ghost and power and went about doing good and healing all oppressed by the devil. (See Acts 10:38.)

You also have this anointing which breaks every yoke and removes every burden. *"And it shall be in that day that the burden of [the Assyrian] shall depart from your shoulders, and his yoke from your neck. The yoke shall be destroyed because of fatness [which prevents it from going around your neck"* (Isaiah 10:27).

Jezebel Spirit

This is a major spirit in our world today as the result of the previous activities of Queen Jezebel. She was the wicked wife of King Ahab of Israel who used his weakness to control him as well as the nation. She was able to subdue and dominate using controlling demonic thoughts.

This is very commonly found in religious non-Christian circles. It is a product of the flesh that opens the door to an evil spirit and it controls by the use of Domineering, Intimidating, and Manipulative tactics (D.I.M.) we previously mentioned. This behavior can easily operate through a person.

In the church, it disrupts the flow of the Spirit. It is

more than just tempting many people into illicit sexual affairs. These Jezebel spirits can stir up envy, jealousy, gossiping, and slander. The devil, of course, hates the prophetic flow of God because the prophetic ministry demands repentance and removes evil without compromise.

Jezebel wanted to destroy Elijah, the prophet, because his prophetic words came with such creative power that this would render the enemy helpless. In addition, sex was a path to her power and influence.

In these demonic conditions, the person must be willing to brutally face the truth and be open to let God crucify their flesh.

Being subjected to the Holy Spirit on a daily basis will permanently set people free.

Religious Spirit

These religious or evil spirits not only oppose, but counterfeit the work of the Holy Spirit by inspiring loyalty to demonic religious concepts and practices. Their plan is to turn people away from Christ through deception. *"In which at one time you walked [habitually]. You were following the course and fashion of this world [were under the sway of the tendency of this present age], following the prince of the power of the air. [You were obedient to and under the control of] the [demon] spirit that still constantly works in the sons of disobedience [the careless, the rebellious, and the unbelieving, who go against the purposes of God]"* (Ephesians 2:2).

The supernatural power of Satan drives men from worshiping the true God so they can turn their primary affections to false gods and other vain things.

Religious spirits work both outside and inside the church, which accounts for the immense totally unnecessary theological disagreements and appalling relationships that exist in the church instead of the expected spiritual harmony that should prevail.

These people are not aware they have religious spirits. Even if they were informed of the truth, they wouldn't be interested in being free because this spirit actually gives them a spirit of importance as the result of pride, envy and self-righteousness.

This attitude was certainly characteristic of the Scribes and Pharisees who hated Jesus and refused to believe in Him, for if they had, they would have had to humble themselves. The following are characteristics of the work of the Religious Spirits:

1. They believe they are always right, but find fault with others.
2. They only tear down, never build up.
3. They are unable to receive correction and instruction.
4. They claim a false philosophy since they can only listen to man.
5. They believe God appointed them for the purpose of helping others.
6. They are unable to tolerate weaknesses and failures in others.
7. They must always receive recognition.
8. They believe every new move of God is suspicious.

9. They are unable to glory in today, only yesterday.
10. They aren't able to leave their own group and don't expect you to either.

A religious spirit starts out as a human spirit and unless it's controlled it can grow into a demonic spirit with power. When the control is significant, it becomes witchcraft with more demonic activity.

Some people become so good at perfection and control they get into demonic perfection. This is not unlike the obsessive-compulsive person with their persistent activities such as washing their hands on a continuous basis.

The Bible has the answer: *"But He gives us more and more grace (power of the Holy Spirit, to meet this evil tendency and all others fully). That is why He says, God sets Himself against the proud and haughty, but gives grace [continually] to the lowly (those who are humble enough to receive it)"* (James 4:6).

Familiar Spirits

These are rather common in the practice of witchcraft. This evil spirit takes on its own personality and obtains its name because of the familiarity that it develops from the relationship with the person involved. Leviticus 19:31 informs us: *"Turn not to those [mediums] who have familiar spirits or to wizards; do not seek them out to be defiled by them. I am the Lord your God."*

An individual commits spiritual adultery when he or she goes outside their relationship with God to get supernatural knowledge, wisdom, guidance, and even power. For some reason, they need to know about the future. Deception always exists with a person involved with a familiar spirit and often they mistake the demonic spirit for the Holy Spirit.

Here is what the Old Testament reveals about this activity: *"A man or woman who is a medium and has a familiar spirit or is a wizard shall surely be put to death, be stoned with stones; their blood shall be upon them"* (Leviticus 20:27).

Necromancy

This is another deception in which the medium is in contact with a spirit which is familiar with a dead person. The necromancer then appears to have contacted the spirit of that dead person when it is actually the familiar spirit that provides the information and any of the manifestations.

This is what God's Word declares about this harmful exposure in Deuteronomy 18:10:11: *"There shall not be found among you anyone who makes his son or daughter pass through the fire, or who uses divination, or is a soothsayer, or an augur, or a sorcerer, Or a charmer, or a medium, or a wizard, or a necromancer."*

A former business friend let it be known to me about their family meeting in his grandfather's bedroom. His brother was the spokesman because he revealed many "facts" about the grandfather even though the man died when his brother was only three year of age. They didn't understand this familiar spirit was already influencing the lives of this family through channeling.

Channeling is a process whereby an individual (the "channeler") claims to have been invaded by a spirit entity which speaks through the channeler. This has been set up as a popular television show with the speaker revealing information to the members of the audience about those who have died.

Don't be tempted to delve into this area.

Drugs

Many drugs, especially the hallucinatory ones, alter the function of brain cells producing an infinite variety of supposed revelations all fostered by familiar spirits. This is a straight corridor into the demonic realm.

Games and Toys

These can become a powerful influence in growing children as the devil attempts to control their lives. Since parents are their spiritual guardians, they must stay alert and become more vigilant and aware of Satan's tricks. One such game is "Dungeons & Dragons" in which a teenager actually lost his own identity and took on the identity of his familiar spirit.

Imaginary Playmates

These so-called playmates are invisible spirits that can become a companion and a teacher to a child—perhaps as a result of loneliness. This evolves into a relationship with a familiar spirit.

One such tragic case is reported in a young woman who experienced an imaginary playmate in her childhood. She would feel rejection and insecurity. Her playmate was a familiar spirit that assumed various forms and exercised supernatural power including occult phenomena. When she was older, she heard unexplained noises which manifested themselves in her house thought to be explained by a mischievous ghost. She also experienced unsought astral travel (of or related to coming from the stars), and undesired psychic insights.

Ouija Board

This supposedly can provide ready answers to many questions concerning life's future because you're dealing with a familiar spirit. It is obviously very dangerous with great risks involved.

Poltergeist

According to Webster's definition this is a noisy ghost held to be responsibile for mysterious noisy disturbances. It's easy to understand how nightmares can occur in people exposed to this activity. Poltergeist spirits can be invited in by the presence of certain pictures, witchcraft, or occultic material.

Transcendental Meditation

When practiced, this opens a person up to deceiving spirits.

Rock Music

This becomes a religion to the devotees for they usually grow to become very defensive and unteachable. The answer is to accept Christ so they can love God and not allow the Holy Spirit to be replaced with "another spirit" they have become familiar with.

Tattooing

This can result in an allegiance to a deity. Tattooing

and body piercing goes back to pagan idolatry and people need deliverance from some of the pictures, symbols, and especially the destruction to parts of the body. *"You shall not make any cuttings in your flesh for the dead nor print or tattoo any marks upon you; I am the Lord"* (Leviticus 19:28).

Teraphims

These are household images made in the likeness of their deceased ancestors. Those involved in this idolatry believe these human figures and statues represent the spirits of the departed dead. The Bible refers to Rachel stealing Laban's (her father) Teraphim.

Modern Day Curses

The following are the most common modern day curses that need to be brought under control since they are not rooted in the Word of God.

1. Disease

You need to get the Word of God in your heart and speak it out of your lips: *"He sends forth His word and heals them and rescues them from the pit and destruction"* (Psalm 107:20).

2. Adultery

With proper instruction you can be free from adultery: *"For the commandment is a lamp, and the whole teaching [of the law] is light, and reproofs of discipline are the way of life, To keep you from the evil woman, from the flattery of the tongue of a loose woman. Lust not after her beauty in your heart, neither let her capture you with her eyelids"* (Proverbs 6:23-25).

3. Arthritis

Many look on this malady as only a physical infirmity. It is a manifestation that can be transmitted from one generation to another, but I have seen the cycle broken through casting out this condition. As the Bible says, *"Behold, you have instructed many, and you have strengthened the weak hands. Your words have held firm him who was falling, and you have strengthened the feeble knees"* (Job 4:3-4).

Thank God, this can be healed with your words and the authority of the Almighty.

4. Blood Disease

The word of God reverses blood disease: *"And when I passed by you and saw you rolling about in your blood, I said to you in your blood, Live! Yes, I said to you still in your natal blood, Live!"* (Ezekiel 16:6).

5. Bone Disease

Pleasant words are health to the bones. *"Pleasant words are like a honeycomb, sweet to the soul and healing to the bones"* (Proverbs 16:24 NIV).

6. Fear of Man.

When you praise the name of the Lord, you will no longer fear what others may do. *"By [the help of] God I will praise His word; on God I lean, rely, and confidently put my trust; I will not fear. What can man, who is flesh, do to me?"* (Psalm 56:4).

7. Fear of Old Age

If you are righteous, you will be fruitful in your latter years. *"The [uncompromisingly] righteous shall flourish like the palm tree [be long-lived, stately, upright, useful, and fruitful]; they shall grow like a cedar in Lebanon [majestic, stable, durable, and incorruptible]... [Growing in grace] they shall still bring forth fruit in old age; they shall be full of sap [of spiritual vitality] and [rich in the] verdure [of trust, love, and contentment]"* (Psalm 92:12,14).

8. Mental Problems

A person who needs to be delivered of this must get the Word into their mind to reverse their mental disorder. *"Roll your works upon the Lord [commit and trust them wholly to Him; He will cause your thoughts to become agreeable to His will, and] so shall your plans be established and succeed"* (Proverbs 16:3).

9. Poverty

When Adam sinned, he changed gods and as a result we lost our incredible wealth—causing poverty to be birthed in humanity. However, the tithe was established to restore the loss of wealth which you are now taking back through Jesus. *"This Book of the Law shall not depart out of your mouth, but you shall meditate on it day and night, that you may observe and do according to all that is written in it. For then you shall make your way prosperous, and then you shall deal wisely and have good success"* (Joshua 1:8).

10. Rebellious Children

The Lord tells us we have to cease from weeping and instead pray, seek Him, and call out for Him. Then He will bring our children back from Satan's territory. *"Thus says the Lord: Restrain your voice from weeping and your eyes from tears, for your work shall be rewarded, says the Lord; and [your children] shall return from the enemy's land"* (Jeremiah 31:16).

The Hippocratic Oath

In my medical school, the Hippocratic Oath was considered a rite of passage for all practitioners of medicine. It was written by Hippocrates in the fourth century BC. However, when I came across it once again, long being a doctor, I was both surprised and upset that I spoke an oath and prayed to gods that apparently were contradictory to the Bible.

Just for your review, here's the first part that was originally translated from the Greek: *"I swear by Asclepius, Hygieia, and Panacea, and I take to witness all the gods, all the goddesses, to keep according to my ability and my judgment, the following Oath."*

Here's what I found in my research. To begin with, Jesus said, *"Do not bind yourself by an oath at all"* (Matthew 5:34).

Then I read in Exodus 23:13, that you shall not violate God's instructions: *"In all I have said to you take heed; do not mention the name of other gods [either in blessing or cursing]; do not let such speech be heard from your mouth.*

Here is an up-to-date modern version of the oath—not the original one I swore by upon entering and leaving medical school:

I swear to fulfill, to the best of my ability and judgment, this covenant: I will respect the hard-won scientific gains of those physicians in whose steps I walk, and gladly share such knowledge as is mine with those who are to follow. I will apply, for the benefit of the sick, all measures [that] are required, avoiding those twin traps of over treatment and therapeutic nihilism.

I will remember that there is art to medicine as well as science, and that warmth, sympathy, and understanding may outweigh the surgeon's knife or the chemist's drug. I will not be ashamed to say "I know not," nor will I fail to call in my colleagues when the skills of another are needed for a patient's recovery.

I will respect the privacy of my patients, for their problems are not disclosed to me that the world may know. Most especially must I tread with care in matters of life and death. If it is given me to save a life, all thanks. But it may also be within my power to take a life; this awesome responsibility must be faced with great humbleness and awareness of my own frailty. Above all, I must not play at God.

I will remember that I do not treat a fever chart, a cancerous growth, but a sick human being, whose illness may affect the person's family and economic stability. My responsibility includes these related problems, if I am to care adequately for the sick. I will prevent disease whenever I can, for prevention is preferable to

> *cure. I will remember that I remain a member of society, with special obligations to all my fellow human beings, those sound of mind and body as well as the infirm.*
>
> *If I do not violate this oath, may I enjoy life and art, respected while I live and remembered with affection thereafter. May I always act so as to preserve the finest traditions of my calling and may I long experience the joy of healing those who seek my help."*

This modern day oath was written in 1964 by Louis Lasagna, the Academic Dean of the School of Medicine at Tufts University and is used throughout many medical schools today.

When you read the current thoughts of many actively practicing physicians on the Internet, there is significant controversy with many contradictory opinions regarding the necessity of agreeing with some of these statements or from even using this oath.

There are undoubtedly many positive aspects in this up-to-date version, but I am concerned for potential abuse concerning the words *"it may also be within my power to take a life."*

I recommend, instead, you just follow Jesus and avoid oaths.

Hospice

Here's what appears to be obviously good news. The work of Hospice and its mission throughout the world has been tremendous. Their goal is to bring high quality palliative care for both patients and families. Their desire is to help alleviate the physical and emotional suffering that has plagued the world from incurable sicknesses and diseases with its tragic consequences.

They have an organized system that functions by promoting communication, facilitating, and providing education, and by becoming an information resource for patients, professionals, health care providers, and policy makers around the world.

Here's the unfortunate truth about the good news. It's not all good, because many of these patients don't have to die. God's reign of glory not only continues to manifest itself upon the human race but is increasing in these end days. Documented testimonies of creative miracles abound, including being brought back from death.

Ignorance of the spiritual realm has brought eternal disaster to many of these patients who have been scheduled or predicted to die, but not intentionally, by the speaking of negative confessions by their health care providers. I never allowed myself to take such a class because it can become habit forming and embarrassing. For example, one woman was in a coma for almost a week and was scientifically deteriorating until her daughter placed an anointed prayer cloth on her head. The woman woke up and was soon discharged.

As a medical doctor, I never questioned the necessity to call upon the consulting expertise of other specialists for my patients' needs, for I was never ashamed to reveal my ignorance in these fields. Likewise, not knowing anything about the spiritual realm—such as the spirit or the soul—is really not a great excuse to deny patients from entering eternity in heaven instead of hell.

Whether a health care provider believes or doesn't believe, does not really matter since the possibility exists. And speaking salvation to the patients is certainly more profound than writing DNR (Do Not Resuscitate) on the chart. What I'm saying is that hospice could be the last chance to save a dying patient. Besides, this is a truth that has already been proven and demonstrated by God literally raising people from the dead.

With the prayer of salvation they can be directed to heaven. The tragedy of not receiving healing and deliverance before their last days is one reason for this handbook. There is no excuse for people not being given the opportunity to live in heaven for eternity since this is their last stay here on earth. Further, there is an unfounded impression that as we reach an advanced age that sickness and disease is supposed to accompany us. You would do well not to speak this into existence.

God is no respecter of persons and if Moses could start his ministry at the age of eighty and live to the ripe old age of 120 with keen eye sight and be strong enough to climb a mountain, so could you. But you won't have to ascend a mountain unless you want to!

RICH REWARDS

I believe doctors are the servants and handmaidens of God who will help usher in the end-time revival that will bring this whole age to a glorious close. You are the ones experiencing the great outpouring of God's Spirit. He is releasing to you His power through Spirit-inspired words of prophecy and prayer with signs, miracles, and wonders following you.

You will be involved in what God is doing in this hour as His bond slave, available to do His bidding 24 hours a day. This is no different than what you have been doing throughout your entire medical career. It's a demanding role, but the rewards are rich. You will be God's mouthpiece here on the earth in these final days as key players in the Holy Spirit's greatest earthly production—preparing people for heaven.

NINE

FROM BONDAGE TO DELIVERANCE

The path from captivity to liberty involves casting out demonic spirits wherever they are found. Let me share seven stages that lead from regression to total possession.

Stage One: Regression

People often revert to earlier behaviors they knew prior to salvation—actions they had been freed from. However, rather than progress forward they start reaching toward habits of the past. There are negative activities which begin to hinder normal expressions and old behaviors become more prevalent. For example, they may use filthy language and tell off-color jokes from their earlier life.

Stage Two: Repression

This level is easy to miss because the steps are so slight, but it becomes more evident that feelings are held back. Restraint is apparent. They murmur and complain more about troubles and problems.

In addition, they reduce their conversation about the Lord and may even show anger and hostility toward God for the circumstances they are going through.

What is the answer? *"He must correct his opponents with courtesy and gentleness, in the hope that God may grant that they will repent and come to know the Truth [that they will perceive and recognize and become accurately acquainted with and acknowledge it]"* (2 Timothy 2:25).

Stage Three: Suppression

They become inactive, listless, slower, have less energy and enthusiasm, and definitely lose interest in their environment. They begin to conceal things, show little desire in their activities and their life, and have no need to discuss their experiences with the Lord. God becomes a secret. Suppression is like being pressed down, squeezed, and crushed.

Stage Four: Depression

Their spiritual level of activity is markedly reduced. They demonstrate rejection, sadness, inactivity, hopelessness, and inadequacy. Withdrawal is apparent. Talking stops. There is fear, separation from others, self-pity, extreme quietness, and staring into space. There is no joy or faith.

Such people prefer to stay alone. They can deal with the first three steps, but if they're going to resist the devil they have to become well balanced. They need to get their will activated and start praising and worshiping the Lord and doing the spiritual things of God to lift this depression from their life.

Stage Five: Oppression

This is serious because there are things that will weigh them down to the point they are unable to maintain their responsibilities. Sickness and disease can occur along with fear, and other unfortunate circumstances. They are overpowered by Satan with feelings of being crushed, overwhelmed, ravaged, and smothered. *"And that they may come to their senses [and]escape out of the snare of the devil, having been held captive by him, [henceforth] to do His [God's]will"* (2 Timothy 2: 26).

Stage Six: Obsession

They become obsessed with the wrong things and require help at this point in order to be set free. They are unreasonable, often lie, and can even become obsessed with a spirit of jealousy. They are unable to deliver themselves. In addition, they can become fixed on a single or unreasonable idea because their mind is not clear and actually they are in bondage. In truth, they are besieged by evil spirits.

Stage Seven: Possession

This is a long step from obsession. Even though there are those who actually become possessed, they have to enter a terrible state before reaching this stage. Now they are completely under the control of the demon. Their own personality is no longer visible. Others can see demonic activity in their eyes. There is total control and rule by extraneous forces with domination.

You can see that Satan attempts to devour the person

a little bit at a time. The key is to resist the devil at the very onset: *"Be well balanced (temperate, sober of mind), be vigilant and cautious at all times; for that enemy of yours, the devil, roams around like a lion roaring [in fierce hunger], seeking someone to seize upon and devour. Withstand him; be firm in faith [against his onset—rooted, established, strong, immovable, and determined], knowing that the same (identical) sufferings are appointed to your brotherhood (the whole body of Christians) throughout the world"* (1 Peter 5: 8-9).

YOUR SPIRITUAL ARMOR

God's armor is one of the many blessings He has given you for the phenomenal spiritual protection of your body. Scripture describes how you can utilize your spiritual armor against demonic spirits.

Learn how to put on and wear these pieces of spiritual clothing by faith so you can avoid encountering demonic spiritual challenges. Then watch how you stand your ground and confirm your victory in Christ Jesus rather than allow your door to open and become another casualty.

We are told:

> *Therefore put on God's complete armor, that you may be able to resist and stand your ground on the evil day [of danger], and, having done all [the crisis demands], to stand [firmly in your place]. Stand therefore [hold your ground], having tightened the belt of truth around your*

loins and having put on the breastplate of integrity and of moral rectitude and right standing with God, And having shod your feet in preparation [to face the enemy with the firm-footed stability, the promptness, and the readiness produced by the good news] of the Gospel of peace.

Lift up over all the [covering] shield of saving faith, upon which you can quench all the flaming missiles of the wicked [one]. And take the helmet of salvation and the sword that the Spirit wields, which is the Word of God.

Pray at all times (on every occasion, in every season) in the Spirit, with all [manner of] prayer and entreaty. To that end keep alert and watch with strong purpose and perseverance, interceding in behalf of all the saints (God's consecrated people) (Ephesians 6:13-18).

This defense against demonic activity is illustrated with the following:

1. The helmet of salvation.

This covers your head and protects your mind. You have victory and you can state that: "I have the mind of Christ with His wisdom and revelation to deal with every issue regardless of its nature."

2. The breastplate of righteousness.

When you put this on you are in right standing with God. You can proclaim: "My heart is protected and made innocent of sin and I'm holy through the cross and the shed blood of Jesus Christ."

Righteousness means "right doing," which is a condition of the heart.

3. Loins girt about with the belt of truth.

This protects you against trials and tribulations from the devil. I believe, "My God is faithful and I will not suffer to be tempted or accept the lies of the enemy as I speak the truth which is the Word of God."

4. Feet shod with the preparation of the gospel of peace.

Put on these shoes which are eager to go willingly wherever He sends you so you can evangelize the world. Claim these words: "The Lord Jesus will lead me so that I will bring peace, fellowship, joy, and glad tidings of good things to all the situations with which I'm dealing."

5. The shield of faith.

During our first day of medical school, the professor announced that we, the students, had to make a decision to believe everything they told us. Simply stated, we weren't going to find time to research everything we heard, but rather we had to just accept it all. It took me many years before I grasped that they were actually teaching us faith without ever using the faith word.

Your shield of faith is built upon the Word of God for this will stop the enemy's burning arrows from piercing you. I insist that: "Every time I read the Word of God or sit under the teaching of the Word, my shield of faith grows larger."

6. The sword of the Spirit.

This weapon will withstand and slay the enemy because the Word of God is sharper than a two-edged sword. I stress that: "As I commit Scriptures to memory, they will appear to me in troubled times and cut through any challenges as a powerful and mighty weapon."

The Word of God is the only offensive weapon to conquer the devil.

7. Prayer and supplication.

Praying in the Spirit makes good sense for it is one of the ways to release the will of God upon the earth. I always say, "My communication with God is strengthened by perseverance, thanksgiving, and praise and I believe that strongholds in the heavenlies are broken."

We are told: *"Be unceasing in prayer [praying perseveringly]"* (1Thessalonians 5:17).

I hope you realize that there is no armor to protect your back simply because God expects you to be facing the enemy at all times, that is, you're always moving forward attacking your adversary.

DETHRONING THE DEVIL

When you walk into a room with a person who needs deliverance, learn how to show up with an attitude of power. Don't be surprised to hear growling and barking demons when you arrive, which confirms why the demons flee from you.

Your job is to dethrone the evil that exists—which comes from the devil. Since you are always in warfare with him, you are advised to constantly be on the offensive rather than the defensive and not tolerate or even refer to his so-called "attacks."

You deliver men and women from demonic activity when you bring God on the scene and they retreat: *"But if it is by the Spirit of God that I drive out the demons, then the kingdom of God has come upon you [before you expected it]"* (Matthew 12:28).

There is a simple way to handle the devil from getting into your thoughts according to Scripture: *"[Inasmuch as we] refute arguments and theories and reasonings and every proud and lofty thing that sets itself up against the [true] knowledge of God; and we lead every thought and purpose away captive into the obedience of Christ (the Messiah, the Anointed One)"* (2 Corinthians 10:5).

DISCOVER THE TRUTH

Those who are in opposition to the truth need to open their hearts so they can receive repentance. *"He must correct his opponents with courtesy and gentleness, in the hope that God may grant that they will repent and come to know the Truth [that they will perceive and recognize and become accurately acquainted with and acknowledge it], And that they may come to their senses [and] escape out of the snare of the devil, having been held captive by him, [henceforth] to do His [God's] will"* (2 Timothy 2: 25-26).

Recovery becomes evident to the captives when they discover the truth of the Word which releases them from bondage so they can keep the commandments: *"Whoever observes the [king's] command will experience no harm, and a wise man's mind will know both when and what to do"* (Ecclesiastes 8:5).

By taking hold of the Word of God they greatly reduce the risk of ever returning to that path again. This consequently enables them to establish a safeguard to protect others.

KEYS OF THE KINGDOM

The prayer given by Jesus involving the power of binding and loosing is spiritual in both the earth and in heaven. This power gives you the opportunity to handle all situations through the Holy Spirit. You will have no more barriers between heaven and earth or between earth and heaven because you now have the keys that make it possible Just claim what you want and it will be done and simply believe it by your faith. *"I will give you the keys of the kingdom of heaven; and whatever you bind (declare to be improper and unlawful) on earth must be what is already bound in heaven; and whatever you loose (declare lawful) on earth must be what is already loosed in heaven"* (Matthew 16:19).

The greatest success for you and those you are trying to help is to accomplish the will of God.

YOUR WEAPONS

Allow me to share eight incredible weapons that are available for you to utilize in times of challenge:

1. Prayer
2. Praise
3. Preaching

4. Your testimony
5. The Word of God
6. The name of Jesus
7. The blood of Jesus
8. Scriptures

Remember: "*So be subject to God. Resist the devil [stand firm against him], and he will flee from you*" (James 4:7).

JESUS DESTROYS SATAN

The Son of God spent more time talking about the devil and hell during His preaching and teaching than healing since He was actively involved in deliverance. In doing so, He was revealing and exposing Satan, not exhorting him.

Jesus came in the flesh as a final sacrifice for your patient's sins, but also to annihilate the works of the devil. As a result of the judgment of Christ when He was nailed to the cross, the prince of this world (who was the ruler of this world) was finally and legally cast out.

The Bible declares, *"Now the judgment (crisis) of this world is coming on [sentence is now being passed on this world]. Now the ruler (evil genius, prince) of this world shall be cast out (expelled)"* (John 12:31).

Yes, it was at the cross that the devil's territory, his authority, and his claims were totally terminated. You can say with complete assurance that the devil was destroyed through the death of Jesus on the cross.

Since this took place, he doesn't need to be defeated any further. It was already done. What we need to do now is to just administer his defeat. *"[But] he who commits sin [who practices evildoing] is of the devil [takes his character from the evil one], for the devil has sinned (violated the divine law) from the beginning. The reason the Son of God was made manifest (visible) was to undo destroy, loosen, and dissolve) the works the devil [has done]"* (1 John 3:8).

Thank God for sending His Son to pay the price for our healing and deliverance at Calvary.

Ten

Sin is Suicide

Never skirt around the issue of sin. It is the core problem of people needing deliverance.

Sin is suicide. It's a violation of what you already know.

The basic motivation producing sin (Self Inflicted Nonsense) is to want to be free or independent of God. Yet, sin gives the devil the legal right to destroy your patients.

We have liberties as the result of our free will, but this means we can yield to temptation even though we don't have to since we are in charge of our flesh. The question to ask the person in need is this: do they want to serve God or do they want to serve the devil?

The sinful mind comes against God: *"[That is] because the mind of the flesh [with its carnal thoughts and purposes] is hostile to God, for it does not submit itself to God's Law; indeed it cannot"* (Romans 8:7).

The devil shows up and enters basically because weakness develops from temptation. That's the time Satan's staff has the opportunity to bind you. He takes advantage of man through the lust of the eye, the lust of the flesh, and the pride of life. The devil sees us as we see ourselves so you need to appreciate that your outward appearance really reflects what's going on in your inside.

Remember, everything the devil does is counterfeit because he is unable to create. He's also an expert on what's legal and what's not for there's no aspect of transgression that is lawful for you.

There is no hope for those who insist in pursuing after sin. Instead, they need to open their heart to the Lord Jesus Christ of Nazareth. Although sin has scars, healing can remove them.

The epitome of the devil's hatred is to give us sickness and disease so he can attack God indirectly by hurting man. He really doesn't care about damaging you because he has no human emotions. He takes advantage of hurting God by harming God's creations. He binds us if we allow him by denying, discrediting, and overcoming the Word we receive.

BREAKING THE CORDS

The wicked man makes a willful choice to sin and so he becomes entrapped in his own iniquities. He is really held by the cords of his sins. The words of his mouth indicate a lack of instruction and understanding which causes him to go astray.

When God's precious Word is lacking, evil usually takes control. One of the keys to deliverance, therefore, is proper instruction. Remember, *"His own iniquities shall ensnare the wicked man, and he shall be held with the cords of his sin"* (Proverbs 5:22).

Thank God, there is total forgiveness: *"If we confess our sins, he is faithful and just to forgive us our sins, and to cleanse us from all unrighteousness"* (1 John 1:9 KJV).

ELEVEN

GOD'S ANOINTING ON YOU

You have been prepared to receive the Lord's anointing so you can and will witness the manifestation of God's awesome healing and deliverance power. The biblical basis for healing is relatively simple. When you speak the name of Jesus, God the Father releases His healing and delivering power, and the anointing of the Holy Spirit comes to work within you on your behalf.

By the anointing, I mean the power to break the yoke (servitude or bondage) and destroy the works of the devil. The Greek word for "power" means "authority." This authority enables us to remove all fleshly and demonic power.

A yoke could be defined as an arched device that was formerly laid on the neck of a defeated person. The anointing, then, is the glory that removes all flesh and all the power of the enemy.

The Bible doesn't require you to become trained as a minister or a pastor; nor does it demand that you enroll in a seminary or Bible school. The only requirement for you to lay hands on the sick and see them recover is for you to be a believer.

Every born again Christian, including you, has been

given authority by God to minister healing to the sick and oppressed. Actually, according to the Bible, the Lord expects you to make the decision to participate as a believer. And when you do, this will happen: *"They shall set their hands on sick men, and they shall wax whole"* (Mark 16:18 Wycliffe New Testament).

TANGIBLE AND TRANSFERABLE

As you absorb this material, you can anticipate the continued release of God's anointing into your spirit for your supernatural, spiritual, understanding power.

There is a spiritual transformation of the Word that you will receive. The Word of God is not just a collection of divinely inspired promises, but a living force that can actually bring the power to make those promises become a reality in your life.

This anointing is both tangible and transferable. Thank God for the scientific approach and the blessings you've experienced and seen come from it, for doctors have utilized this system to care for countless patients throughout the entire world.

Early on, this was the only method I wanted to know about in my practice. When you have been trained in and practiced a certain approach for most of your career, you become totally reliant and dependent upon it. Therefore, why would you want to research or investigate any other form of patient treatment? But when I was healed of an incurable medical condition, I began to wonder, "Could I have been wrong all these years in my medical practice?"

I pray you will discover one of the priceless treasures of my life—God's anointing.

TWELVE

HEARING THE VOICE OF GOD

Here's a question I am constantly asked: "How do you hear the voice of God?"

Let's start with the basics. The first thing you have to believe is that you *can* hear His voice through the mind He has given you.

You may not realize to whom you have been listening, but the truth is that it's both your voice and His voice. The only way to discern the difference is to realize that His voice is always looking for His desires for you and your voice is always looking for your desires for yourself.

God wants you to think and talk about things that are outside your own comforts, boundaries, and limitations. The importance of hearing His voice is for you to be able to pull His desires that are for you out of yourself.

You already have a treasury in you that God placed there. This is why you want to hear His voice.

In reality, there are many ways He communicates with you, probably dependent on your personality and character that He honors.

Every doctor has had challenging medical situations that were properly answered which, as you reflect back, you knew you did not solve. My impression is that God speaks to us all the time provided we are ready and open to hear Him. However, the sound of our voice may not allow Him to get through especially when we are continuously talking. We need to have faith and actually believe it is possible.

Here is one of the many powerful Scriptures that reveals God's presence within us: *"Little children, you are of God [you belong to Him] and have [already] defeated and overcome them [the agents of the antichrist], because He Who lives in you is greater (mightier) than he who is in the world"* (1 John 4:4).

Since the beginning of creation, even before God spoke, the Spirit moved and His pattern has never ceased to change. Through His grace He is living in you.

In order to have an ongoing relationship with God, it is vital to hear His voice. This is summed up in Jeremiah 7:23: *"But this thing I did command them: Listen to and obey My voice, and I will be your God and you will be My people; and walk in the whole way that I command you, that it may be well with you."*

This is also confirmed in the New Testament, for hearing His voice is the mark of a true disciple. *"The sheep that are My own hear and are listening to My voice; and I know them, and they follow Me"* (John 10:27).

Faith comes when you hear His voice every day, for it provides you with direction and strength. Hearing actually comes through an inner condition of the heart—known as a hearing heart—which you can ask God for.

To get this sensitivity of the heart to hear His voice correctly, four things are required:

1. Undivided attention.
2. Humility (obedience).
3. Time.
4. Quietness.

The best preparation for this is with worship: *"O come, let us worship and bow down, let us kneel before the Lord out Maker [in reverent praise and supplication]"* (Psalm 95:6).

The evidence that you heard the voice of God:

1. There is agreement with Scripture (which comes from the Holy Spirit) and its principles.
2. There will be confirmation of the circumstances in one way or another.
3. God's peace resides in your heart.
4. There will be confirmation through fellow believers.

"JESUS LOVES YOU"

May I suggest that when something happens that appears to be perfect timing that you are referring to as a coincidence, take a moment to reconsider that it was God.

Here is a great example of hearing the voice of God and confirmation of the circumstances.

I met a nurse in the hospital with a hardened spirit. We would pass each other in the hospital hallways and talk briefly, but apparently whatever I said would upset her. So, to break that hardness, I knew to tell her, "Jesus loves you." I suspected that was the Holy Spirit.

One time we saw each other at a mall and she confronted me, "I am upset that you prayed for my mother, and she didn't like it either."

I attempted to apologize, but that seemed to make matters worse. She wouldn't listen because she said my praying should have never happened in the first place. Again, I heard to tell her, "Jesus loves you."

Indignantly, she told me to stop saying that because she didn't believe it.

About a week later, I heard from a close friend of hers in the hospital that as she was driving out of state, her eyes caught a large billboard that read, "Jesus loves you" after which she couldn't stop crying.

God has ways of speaking to us.

THIRTEEN

CASTING OUT DEMONS

When it is necessary to cast out demonic spirits from your patients, if there is any question in your mind, just tell them to come out in the name of Jesus without causing any harm and then send them to "dry places." This is a biblical term referenced below.

You can also command them to be bound to the cord of the Holy Spirit and sent to the pit. Some command they be sent to the abyss, but dry places are an agreeable place to go. They are not in hell as yet so don't bother sending them there.

When spirits are cast out following deliverance, unless the "clean house" of that person is maintained and replaced with spiritual knowledge, which involves reading the Word, memorizing Scriptures, honoring God, and removing all the old junk which caused the problem in the first place, the demons often return to seek reentrance into their old home and reestablish their demonic ways. This is quite obvious from reading Matthew 12:43-45: *"But when the unclean spirit has gone out of a man, it roams through dry [arid] places in search of rest, but it does not find any. Then it says, I will go back to my house from which I came out. And when it arrives, it finds the place unoccupied, swept, put in order, and decorated. Then it goes and brings with it seven other spirits more wicked than itself, and they go in and make their home there. And the last condition of that man becomes worse than the first. So also shall it be with this wicked generation."*

Thank God for the power of the Word with this awesome description as described in Jeremiah 23:29: *"'Is not My word like a fire?' says the Lord, 'And like a hammer that breaks the rock in pieces?'"*

DELIVERANCE FROM EVIL SPIRITS

When you deal with a demonic situation, find the seed of the problem and depend on your gift of discernment. Ask multiple questions to your patient until you get a clue or a handle as to how this started. Don't forget that rejection is a common root.

Encourage your patient to consider prayer and fasting prior to your meeting. Again, refer to their deliverance as removing "bad" or evil spirits rather than initially informing them that they have a demon.

PREPARATION FOR DELIVERANCE

1. Give up sin; otherwise this becomes an open invitation to demons. Yielding to the devil is spiritual death. Obedience leads to righteousness or right standing with God.
2. Get into repentance.

3. Forgiveness is absolutely necessary.
4. Cast out pride so they don't have to deal with the lust of the eyes, the lust of the flesh, and the pride of life.
5. Total separation is necessary. Give up anything and everything connected with the occult, and cults, and destroy any and all materials associated with this. Clean their house, their room, their drawers, etc. Destroy demonic pictures, materials, images, including pornography.

INDICATIONS FOR DELIVERANCE

1. Deep-seeded emotional situations.
2. Mental challenges from your thoughts.
3. Significant speech challenges.
4. Deep-seeded sexual challenges.
5. Addictions and compulsions.
6. Physical infirmities.
7. False religious beliefs.
8. Roaming about without purpose.

KEYS TO DELIVERANCE

1. Renouncing the problem.
2. Calling on the Lord.
3. Obeying the Word.
4. Ceasing demonic activity.
5. Fully repenting.

SOLUTIONS TO DELIVERANCE

1. Honesty will expose demonic activity that the Holy Spirit will remove.
2. Humility will reduce pride so you can be filled with the Holy Spirit.
3. Reverence (fear) and respect for God develops a hatred for improper behavior.
4. Love of God will cause your love for things of the world to be purged.
5. Renounce sin and the kingdom of darkness for this will destroy a lifestyle of iniquity including associations with the wrong people.
6. Forgiveness of all offenses, both of yours and others, to produce a new you.
7. Enter into warfare against the devil, and command the demon spirits to leave by name.
8. Submit to the authority of God, the blood of Jesus, the Word of God, and the leading of the Holy Spirit.
9. Put God first in your life.

FOURTEEN

7 FUNDAMENTAL BIBLICAL REVELATIONS FOR HEALING AND DELIVERANCE

Healing and deliverance have always been expressions of the character of God. The biblical basis for this divine work is relatively simple. When you speak the name of Jesus, the Father, God, releases the power and the anointing of the Holy Spirit to work on your behalf. His divine workmanship comes into operation for you as you walk with Him.

Let me speak to those who are not health professionals. You may be thinking, "But, I have no medical training." However, you can read and understand spiritual laws. In addition, although you've never been in a medical school classroom, you can lay hands on the sick, utilizing these principles and participate in their full recovery. (See Mark 16:18.)

Healing is absolutely based on a covenant from God

that is found in the Old Testament: *"And the Lord said, Behold, I lay down [afresh the terms of the mutual agreement between Israel and Me] a covenant. Before all your people I will do marvels (wonders, miracles) such as have not been wrought or created in all the earth or in any nation; and all the people among whom you are shall see the work of the Lord; for it is a terrible thing [fearful and full of awe] that I will do with you"* (Exodus 34:10).

Jesus has given us the responsibility of ministering His healing and delivering power to the sick and oppressed so they can stay healed and remain free from Satan's bondage. Plus, He wants us to teach others how to heal and deliver.

The plan of God is to uplift Jesus, so He can draw all men to Him. The Great Commission—the last words Jesus spoke on Earth—informs us of what we are required to do here and now:

> *"And He said to them, Go into all the world and preach and publish openly the good news (the Gospel) to every creature [of the whole human race]. He who believes [who adheres to and trusts in and relies on the Gospel and Him Whom it sets forth] and is baptized will be saved [from the penalty of eternal death]; but he who does not believe [who does not adhere to and trust in and rely on the Gospel and Him Whom it sets forth] will be condemned. And these attesting signs will accompany those who believe: in My name they will drive out demons; they will speak in new languages; They will pick up serpents; and [even]*

if they drink anything deadly, it will not hurt them; they will lay their hands on the sick, and they will get well" (Mark 16:15-18).

PREPARATION FOR MIRACLES

Jesus was a believer and doer of the full gospel, which involves preaching, teaching, healing, and deliverance. The truth is that the ministry of the gospel must include demonstration—for this brings completion to the full gospel.

In studying the Word, I developed seven key, fundamental biblical revelations from the Bible. I extracted them, focused on them, magnified them, applied them, experienced them, and finally watched them work quite successfully. You will receive the same spiritual revelations that are based on biblical principles.

You don't need doctor experience if you just rely on the Holy Spirit along with the Word of God which is already in your heart. Again, you didn't miss out by not going to medical school or into the ministry. These instructions are easier "caught than taught," and this happens as Jesus Christ of Nazareth uses you as a yielded vessel.

Remember, to live by revelation knowledge instead of sense knowledge you should only be moved by what you believe, not by what you see, feel, hear, taste, touch, or smell, because this is without faith. Stop talking only about the way things are. You cannot deal in the supernatural realm if you are relying on your soul, your body, your five physical senses, or your logic. You will receive unshakable confidence from these revelations, so that the gates of hell cannot prevail against you. As Scripture states, *"I will build My church, and the gates of Hades (the powers of the infernal region) shall not overpower it [or be strong to its detriment or hold out against it]"* (Matthew 16:18).

God's theology says that as a believer you have already received the authority and dominion to enable you to apply Mark 16:18: *"They will lay their hands on the sick, and they will get well."* You have the ability to anticipate and witness miracles, signs, and wonders, and to help people with sicknesses and diseases, especially those who may lack belief, which means they really are full of doubt and undeveloped faith.

The truth is that Jesus has already healed and delivered you; He did so when He died on the cross for your sins and your sicknesses. You are no longer struggling to get healed, for you have already been healed in the supernatural, but rather, you are fighting to maintain your healing and deliverance.

Never forget: *"At all times and for everything giving thanks in the name of our Lord Jesus Christ to God the Father"* (Ephesians 5:20).

Before the healing takes place, create a spiritual atmosphere and pray the following prayer of salvation that they can repeat out loud as you say it:

> *"Lord Jesus, I need You. Thank You for dying on the cross for my sins. I open the door of my heart and life and receive You as my Lord and Savior. Thank You for forgiving my sins and giving me eternal life. Take control of my life and make me the kind of person You want me to be."*

7 FUNDAMENTAL BIBLICAL REVELATIONS

1. Control Your Tongue

Let's begin with this premise: according to the Bible, there is absolutely nothing wrong with you. You need to accept this truth, because Jesus told us to say what you want rather than to say what you have, according to Romans 4:17: *"Who gives life to the dead and speaks of the nonexistent things that [He has foretold and promised] as if they [already] existed."* God, who brings the dead back to life, can bring into existence what didn't exist before.

It's vital to understand that what you say is what you get. This means that what you confess is what you possess. In the supernatural world, when you speak negative confessions, you bring demonic spirits into your atmosphere and you can actually usher in the reality of what you said into existence. How you run or control your mouth is reflected in how you run or control your life.

We are speaking words that agree with the Word of God, words that ignore your circumstances. You're speaking the truth in advance and speaking through your spirit rather than your mind. This amounts to speaking by faith, which is really an acronym that is formed by these words: Fantastic Adventures In Trusting Him. This applies to expressions such as this one, which I've heard a few times: "Doc, every December, like clockwork, I get pneumonia. This pain comes and goes."

I asked, "Then, why do you schedule it?"

You see, words have power, and they can effect changes in all aspects of our life. Therefore, speak positive confessions. For healing to take place through the angels, bring your words into the realm of spiritual reality. Otherwise, it will take thirteen positives to overcome one negative.

2. Jesus Already Healed You on the Cross

When Jesus died on the cross and took upon Himself every medical condition that ever existed, this included diabetes, heart disease, high blood pressure, obesity, pain, colds, accidents, etc.

The question is: how could you have any of these if He took them? They're all listed under the category of sicknesses and diseases in the Bible, each and every one. It also applies to your deliverance.

He was the only Man who never had a sickness or disease until He went to the cross, and then He nailed every one of them to the tree, so you wouldn't have to bear them. *"And thus He fulfilled what was spoken by the prophet Isaiah, He Himself took [in order to carry away] our weaknesses and infirmities and bore away our diseases"* (Matthew 8:17).

Isaiah prophesied that Jesus would not be recognized on the cross, because—through His suffering—He was severely tortured—He took all of our sicknesses and diseases: *"[For many the Servant of God became an object of horror; many were astonished at Him.] His face and His whole appearance were marred more than any man's, and His form beyond that of the sons of men—but just as many were astonished at Him"* (Isaiah 52:14).

He actually took every sickness and disease when He received such an inhumane and torturous beating. I can't image why He wanted to substitute His body for you and me, but He endured it so we wouldn't have to. The Scriptures memorialized this sacrifice in Isaiah 53:5: *"But He was wounded for our transgressions, He was bruised for our guilt and iniquities; the chastisement [needful to obtain] peace and well-being for us was upon Him, and with the stripes [that wounded] Him we are healed and made whole."*

3. God is Greater than Medical Facts

The place of agreement is the place of power. Jesus pointed this out in Matthew 18:19: *"Again I tell you, if two of you on earth agree (harmonize together, make a symphony together) about whatever [anything and everything] they may ask, it will come to pass and be done for them by My Father in heaven."*

The doctor will bring you up to date by showing you every one of the facts and results from all the tests in your medical chart. But listen to this first! Facts themselves are unreliable, unstable, undependable, fluctuating, and not constant. All the things I learned in medical school are within the realm of facts; and because they are facts, they keep changing. Jesus sums it up quite accurately by telling you that all facts are made by humans. So, why accept them?

Further, medical diagnoses represent a curse, so don't agree with them in your heart because your authority is really in Jesus who already took them.

Your healing or deliverance really amounts to faith over circumstances. That is, your faith is so strong that it refuses the right of any negative circumstances to exist in your body, even though they may exist outside your body.

In addition, your faith not only denies and ignores the facts, but it can actually change them. This means that so-called facts can become an illusion or an artifact. If the fact is that you limp when you walk and you are healed, those "facts" can no longer exist. For they have disappeared. The truth is that everything in the natural is subject to change.

4. You Have Awesome Power When You Know Who You Are in the Spirit

The reason for this is that the Lord is living inside of you and you are the Kingdom of God. According to Scripture, *"God said, Let Us [Father, Son, and Holy Spirit] make mankind in Our image, after Our likeness, and let them have complete authority over the fish of the sea, the birds of the air, the [tame] beasts, and over all of the earth, and over everything that creeps upon the earth"* (Genesis 1:26).

This is how He did it for you: *"Then the Lord God formed man from the dust of the ground and breathed into his nostrils the breath or spirit of life, and man became a living being"* (Genesis 2:7).

The truth is that the devil knows you're born again, for he can see the Holy Spirit in you. But if you don't realize how much power you really have, the devil can then take advantage of your unawareness and stop you. You must not let this happen.

The legitimacy here is that you have power to stop tornados, hurricanes, to heal and deliver, and even raise the dead. You actually have more power than Niagra Falls, which supplies the East coast with electrical power.

In addition, Galatians 4:7 states that you're an h-e-i-r of God, and the resurrected Christ is living inside you. I have seen people instantly healed and delivered when they were able to grasp the truth that Jesus is living within them, because they (you) are the Kingdom of God.

It's a paradox for Jesus to live in an ill body if the afflicted person is aware of this, because He will destroy sickness and disease if it exists in His presence.

5. Your Spirit is Totally Healthy and Normal

Understand this: If your spirit took one step outside your body so you could observe it, you would find that it is completely healthy and normal, because it is designed by God. This means there can't be any sickness or disease in your body or in heaven. Practically all of our sicknesses and diseases are from the demonic realm.

According to the Word, you have power over your body and the enemy when your spirit takes charge of your flesh (soul and body). You can minister to the spirit with this Scripture, so speak it out loud: *"Behold! I have given you authority and power to trample upon serpents and scorpions, and [physical and mental strength and ability] over all the power that the enemy [possesses]; and nothing shall in any way harm you"* (Luke 10:19).

Again, you have incredible power over both your body and the enemy. Your soul is your will, your mind or intellect, your emotions, and your senses. Do you know, your soul is kind of flakey, fickle, and not very stable? Therefore, don't allow your soul to run the show, because it can be greatly influenced by the devil.

Since not all of your thoughts are from you, be sure to direct the devil to stop (shut up) talking and stop listening to the negative.

6. You Can Talk to Your Body

Please hear this: everything in the supernatural as well as the natural has ears and everything has to obey you. You can command your body to perform by speaking to it with authority and dominion in the mighty name of Jesus! Every tissue in your body has ears and has to obey. A minister named Joyce Gill was adjusting her curtains when the ladder on which she was standing started falling. She immediately spoke and commanded, "Ladder, upright yourself in the name of Jesus." It did!

Jesus taught us to talk to our bodies just like He did when He spoke to the fig tree when He discovered that it had no fruit: *"And as He saw one single leafy fig tree above the roadside, He went to it but He found nothing but leaves on it [seeing that in the fig tree the fruit appears at the same time as the leaves]. And He said to it, Never again shall fruit grow on you! And the fig tree withered up at once"* (Matthew 21:19).

The disciples were surprised that the tree died, especially since it happened so quickly. Jesus was disappointed with His disciples' lack of faith. In truth, you actually have more faith when you're only moved by what you believe and you take your eyes off yourself and the problem: *"And Jesus answered them, Truly I say to you, if you have faith (a firm relying trust) and do not doubt, you will not only do what has been done to the fig tree, but even if you say to this mountain, Be taken up and cast into the sea, it will be done. And whatever you ask for in prayer, having faith and [really] believing, you will receive"* (Matthew 21:21-22).

7. You Can Minister Healing and Deliverance

Become free of hindrances such as these: it's not God's will; I'm not worthy; or it won't work. There is a quick way to resolve unforgiveness, simply use this prayer:

> *"Lord Jesus, thank you for the opportunity and privilege to totally forgive and forget any hurts I may have received from the following people: ______________...and anyone else I may not remember. Now, Lord Jesus, thank you for this release of bondage and any hurts that I may have given to any of them or myself."*

Prepare the people as you minister:

1. Just listen, don't talk—and keep your eyes open.
2. Picture Jesus healing you everywhere you hurt.
3. Give your testimony (a weapon) to believers.
4. Only use past tense to discuss your previous illness.

When you document the results of your ministering and note the pertinent points, be sure to type or write down that the person was "healed." for this will overcome any negativity spoken or recorded on their medical charts. I believe "It is written" is more powerful than "It is spoken."

Let me encourage you to act on these seven fundamental biblical revelations as you minister healing and deliverance to those in need.

FIFTEEN

HEALING AND DELIVERANCE MIRACLES A TO Z

Let me emphasize that almost everyone who requires and is open to healing and deliverance needs to receive and practice the power which has been given to us, including cursing the cells, roots, and seeds, casting out the spirit of infirmity, eliminating the facts, rebuking the medical conditions, and directing the creative miracles.

"I COMMAND!"

Over time you will know and learn the commands needed by your patients or those you are trying to help. They will flow from you almost ad-lib or automatic. For example:

- "I command strength to come back into the legs!"
- "Pain, come out!"

- "All traces of scar tissue, leave!"
- "You devil of blindness, come out!"
- "Devil, I cancel your assignment. I break and destroy your power!"
- "I command you spirit of infirmity to come out now! I rebuke you!"
- "Spirit of anger, I loose you!"
- "You power of witchcraft, go!"
- "I command you to obey me—come out of him now without hurting him!"
- "You deaf and dumb spirit, come out!"
- "I call forth the angelic power to fight for me in the spiritual world."

As you command healing and deliverance, keep including the words "In the name of Jesus."

SPECIFIC PRAYERS

The following prayers will enable you to resolve serious challenges. The key is for the person to be released from demonic activity and be set free by the power of Christ before dealing with the physical elements.

The actual words you use will depend on the individual circumstances in each case. Feel free to design and add any anti-demonic prayer to cover whatever is necessary so the person can be released from that particular situation.

In these commands you can replace all the essential building blocks of the body by speaking them into existence. You can also choose what your patient needs, including commands for creative miracles listed below. You will find the following examples can cover the major aspects that you would need for healing and deliverance.

Before you lay hands to minister, even if it's by the telephone, take advantage of visualization by picturing you having the hands of Christ because of His anointing and complete the healing to the affected areas.

Father, I know you hear us just like you hear your Son Jesus when He prays. Lord, I call attention to your Word in Jeremiah 32:27 that declares: "Behold, I am the Lord, the God of all flesh; is there anything too hard for Me?" You raise people from the dead so this healing is easy for you. Further Lord, you're no respecter of persons since You have healed multitudes of people with the same identical medical conditions and You show no favoritism.

In the name of Jesus, and by the power of the Holy Spirit, I take authority and dominion over any and all demonic spirits and break your power. I cancel any and all of your assignments. I bind, muzzle, loose, and gag you in the mighty name of Jesus.

In the name of Jesus and by the power of the Holy Spirit, I curse any abnormal cells, roots, seeds of these conditions with lying symptoms and signs and command them to come out now. I rebuke them in the name of Jesus. I command any and all spirits of infirmity, unclean spirits, spirits of inheritance and generational curses, and all strongmen to come out now. I cast out any spirits of fear, doubt, stress, strife, anxiety, and depression and I ask you to bind all of these spirits to the cord of the Holy Spirit and send them to the pit.

I command all the chemical, electrical, and magnetic frequencies in each and every cell to return to normal balance and harmony and any and all abnormal cells to be digested by the good cells.

I command a creative miracle in the name of Jesus with new muscles, ligaments, tendons, nerves, tissues, bone, bone marrow, cartilage, meniscus, fascia, joint, all fluids, blood vessels, vertebrae, and discs.

I command a creative miracle in the name of Jesus with total healing from the crown of the head to the tip of the toes, from the crown of the head to the tip of the fingers. I command a creative miracle with all new organs in their body and head and to function in the perfection to which God created it. I command the blood to flow pure and clean.

I command a supernatural immunological system in the name of Jesus to protect them against any further invading alien attacking organisms. I command your brain to send healing signals to the affected areas and be healed.

I command and speak into every cell of their body a spirit of joy, love, truth, and peace above and beyond any human comprehension or understanding. I command sweet sleep to come upon your beloved at night in the name of Jesus.

I decree and declare in the name of Jesus it's done and finished and I seal this prayer with the blood of Jesus in the name of the Father, the Son, and the Holy Spirit in Jesus' name.

MIRACLES A TO Z

Now let's look at specific conditions and how you can minister healing and deliverance.

The majority of these diagnoses I have ministered to, but I have carefully pointed out that according to God's Word they couldn't possibly have any of these conditions since: (1) they don't exist in heaven, only in the demonic realm, (2) Jesus took every one of your sicknesses or diseases (stripes) when He was on the cross, and (3) Jesus desires that you speak to what you want, not what you have, because we call those things which are not as though they were (Romans 4:19).

Doctors and practitioners of faith, I recommend you lead your patients through the seven fundamental biblical revelations (listed in chapter 14) for each and every one of the medical conditions you encounter. Be sure to follow the guiding of the Holy Spirit which may initially seem to be your own thoughts.

After ministering, be sure to demonstrate the person is healed or delivered, even if they are already aware that a transformation has taken place.

Abdominal Discomfort Pain

When a 13-year-old started speaking, "I have no pain," even though she did, the pain vanished.

Abscess Tooth

I prayed, "I command the spirit of infection to come out, the pain to leave, and a creative miracle with a new tooth with a healthy nerve supply." The pain, tenderness, and swelling left.

Achilles Tendonitis

I told one patient, "Place your fingers on the tender area and rebuke the spirit of inflammation." There was no further pain with movement.

Acid Reflux (GERD)

"I curse the cells, roots, and seeds of this condition and command a creative miracle with a new gastrointestinal system." The pain in this person left.

Acne

To a woman with this condition: "I curse the cells, roots, and seeds of these multiple lesions and command them to come out and be replaced with new baby skin and normal hormonal levels." She was vastly improved and had a big smile on her face.

Aging

"Moses was 120 years old when he died; his eye was not dim nor his natural force abated" (Deuteronomy 34:7). He wasn't sick. Why expect sickness and disease at any age; isn't that like scheduling it?

Anointing Oil

It is meaningful to apply the oil by making the cross.

Arterial Disease (Blood Vessel Obstruction)

"I command a divine 'rotor rooter' treatment system with all the vessels to be open and new and free of blockage with normal oxygenation to all the tissues."

Autism

"I command the spirits of autism, inheritance and generational curse to come out. I command normal thought processes and for the brain to retain wisdom and knowledge and bring clarity to the brain."

Addictions

Cast out the spirit of bondage. A drinker released from prison is still open to bondage because that spirit is still in him.

AIDS

"I command this spirit of infection to come out as I curse the demonic spirit of infirmity and rebuke you and command a supernatural immunological system with healthy cells with a new bone marrow. I command every ungodly soul tie spirit to come out and command any damaged, broken, or fragmentation of the soul to be totally restored. I call forth the angels of God to carry this activity out in the name of Jesus."

Allergies

"I curse this spirit of infirmity and rebuke it and command all allergies to come out and for a supernatural immunological system to be present."

Alzheimer's

I ministered to a man in a nursing home with the seven fundamental biblical revelations and expected healing. He showed signs of improvement enough to make occasional visits home. Remember, Jesus took every illness and infirmity with Him to the cross—including Alzheimer's disease.

Amnesia

I commanded a new memory for the brain of a woman from the Dominican Republic and she was dramatically healed.

Amytrophic Lateral Sclerosis, Bulbar *(Lou Gehrig's Disease)*

"I curse the damaged cells, roots, and seeds of all the nerve cells in the lower motor neurons and command them to be totally replaced with healthy cells." I ministered this prayer in English and a Greek woman was healed.

Anemia

"I command a new bone marrow with all new flesh cells, normal production, and total restoration of this person's hematological system."

Angina

"I curse the damage and command a creative miracle with a new heart, new coronary arteries, and no further chest pain."

Ankylosing Spondylitis

"I command the spirit of infirmity to come out and the inflammation, and degeneration, with all new tissues."

Anorexia

"I command the deaf and dumb spirit of this eating disorder to come out in the name of Jesus." The woman I prayed for was healed without further weight concerns.

Arthritis

"I command the spirit of arthritis to come out and pain to leave with a full range of motion of all joints and all new tissue."

Asthma

"I rebuke this asthma and command the spirit of infirmity to come out and I command a creative miracle with new lungs."

Atrial Fibrillation

"I curse the cells, roots, and seeds of any heart damage and a creative miracle; a new heart, a new conduction system, and for the pulse to return to normal with a normal sinus rhythm." I have seen this prayer answered.

Autoimmune

"I curse the cell, roots, and seeds of this overactive immune response activity in the body and command the body to cease and desist in attacking its own cells. I command the spirit of infirmity to come out and a creative miracle with all new tissues."

Baker's Cyst

"I rebuke the cyst and command the swelling and pain to come out."

Baldness

"I command the dead cells to come out and the spirit of life and health to go back into the hair cells. I command normal hair growth with normal hair cells." We have heard amazing reports of the growth of new hair in answer to prayer.

Bells Palsy, Residual

"I curse the source of this impairment and command a creative miracle with a new seventh nerve and all its branches to totally innervate healthy muscles with resulting normal symmetry of the face."

Bipolar Disorder

"I cast the deaf and dumb spirit of this disorder to come out in the name of Jesus." Instant healing occurs.

Biting Demonic Spirit

A woman named Clarita Villaneuva had constant demonic attacks manifested by bite wounds over her entire body in the Bilibid prison in Manila. Lester Sumrall delivered her through Jesus—which led to 150,000 people experiencing salvation as a result of this great miracle.

Bladder Cancer

"I command the foul spirit of cancer to come out and all cancer cells to be consumed. I curse the cells, roots, and seeds and the spirit of fear and command a creative miracle with a new bladder. I assign a permanent memory to the anti-cancer killer attack cells in the body to kill and destroy immediately any new cancer cells." There are countless documented cases of cancer being cured through prayer.

Blephospasm

A 9-year-old girl frequently squeezed her eyelids tightly closed, blinked her eyes, scrunched her nose up, twisted her mouth, pulled her shoulders up, and moved her neck backwards, all without control. The demonic spirit of infirmity was cast out and she stopped the movements.

Blind Eye, Left, Diabetic Retinopathy

"I command the spirit of infirmity to come out in the name of Jesus and for a creative miracle with new eyes, sclera, cornea, conjunctiva, lens, pupils, retina, optic discs, optic nerves, macula, fovea, cones, rods, fluid, normal blind spot, normal pressure, blood vessels, extraocular muscles, and 20/20 vision." This prayer resulted in vision being returned to normal in both eyes of the person we prayed for.

Brachial plexus Traction Palsy

"I curse this spirit and any damage to the tissues, and

command the nerves, muscles, ligaments, and tendons to return to normal length and strength as well as normal sensation. The spirit of trauma come out."

Brain, Neurologically Impaired

Healing evangelist Charles Hunter had to crawl under a table to touch a child's head who then told his mom he got a "new brain." Several years later, this now older boy saw Charles at a meeting and confirmed his total healing.

Brain Swelling With Pseudotumor Cerebri

The source of a young slightly-overweight woman's impairment was commanded to come out and the cerebral spinal fluid production to return to normal in the name of Jesus. Her unreliable "lying" symptoms resolved.

Brain Tumor, Malignant *(Glioblastoma multiforme)*

"I cast out this spirit of infirmity and rebuke it in the name of Jesus." I prayed this for a man and his visual impairment, cognitive, and balance impairment totally recovered. In addition, his bone flap from the craniotomy was no longer moveable. The repeat MRI was dramatically improved. Of course, the clinic told him that medication was responsible for his remission.

Breast Cyst

To a woman with this condition: "I command this breast

cyst to come out in the name of Jesus." At the doctor's office, the cyst was no longer palpable and the MRI and needle biopsy was cancelled.

Breast Mass

A woman with a breast mass was attending a healing meeting where another person was being prayed for. When she heard the words, "I command that lump to break loose and come out of her," she suddenly felt the lump in her own breast disappear because of the power of her faith.

Bronchitis

A woman had a colorless productive sputum and a persistent cough. "I command the spirit of infection come out in the name of Jesus and for new lungs, bronchi, and alveoli." Her congestion cleared immediately.

Bursitis

"I command the spirit of bursitis to come out of a woman, for the pain to leave, and a creative miracle with all new tissues." She had a full range of motion of her shoulder without further pain or any area of tenderness.

Cancer, embyronal tumor

I ministered to a 7-year-old boy with a diagnosis of rhabdomyosacroma before chemotherapy was started. I learned the doctors were amazed that all of his tumors disappeared after one treatment. Cancelling further chemotherapy was between God and the parents.

Cancer of the Liver

I ministered to a woman with inoperable cancer in my healing room (living room). She vomited large pieces of black and gray material without form into a flower pot which became an emergency emesis basin. She became asymptomatic and left without pain.

Cancer, Pancreas

A woman with this condition was healed, but her health care provider advised her otherwise—which is how the devil attempted to steal her healing. Further ministering resolved this and she was thanking Jesus for her healing.

Cancer, Stomach

Kenneth Copeland reported: "The first lady we came to had weighed less than 80 pounds and the picture of death. I walked over toward her and before I could open my mouth, I heard a voice from behind me say, 'In the Name of Jesus, take up your bed and walk.' She instantly spit up that cancer onto the floor and jumped off that bed and screamed, 'I'm healed,' and started running around the room. Healing is the finished work of Jesus. We have the power to set people free."

Cancer, Time to Stop The Medication

On the television program, "This is Your Day," a man, healed of cancer, experienced sensations of pins and needles throughout his body. Then he saw the thick jar of medication had split open and as it was dripping out. He knew God wanted him to stop taking it.

Cancer of the Tongue

"I command the spirit of cancer to come out and for all pain to go. I curse the cells, roots, and seeds of this damage and command a creative miracle with all new tissues including a new tongue."

Carpal Tunnel Syndrome, Bilateral

I ministered to a nurse by placing my thumbs at the base of her wrists and commanded the carpal tunnel to open up, and for the muscles, ligaments, tendons, and nerves to return to normal length and strength and for any swelling or edema to come out. Her strength returned without any further numbness.

Cataract

"I command the spirit of blindness to come out, cloudy material in the lens to dissolve and melt away, and for the protein content and drying effect of the tissue to be restored with 20/20 vision."

Celiac Disease

"I curse the cells, roots, and seeds, and bind the spirit of infirmity. I command absorption of all nutrients to be normal and to absorb gluten without any impairment. I command a creative miracle with a new immunological system, GI tract, and especially normal villi."

Cervical Disc With Radiculopathy

"I command the pressure on the nerve roots from the herniated disc to come out and be free of swelling, fibrosis, adhesions, or scarring. I command the radiculopathy to leave."

Cervical and Lumbar Sprains

"I command the pain to come out and all the muscles to relax without any further muscle spasm. I command a full range of motion of the neck and lumbosacral spine."

Children, Deliverance

I minister to the parents since they are responsible and accountable for their children. The devil can use a tactic causing the child to scream as you come closer and if sympathy is achieved, the deliverance will be terminated. Command the devil to "Loose them in the name of Jesus." A child that sees monsters and ugly creatures at night is likely experiencing a demonic spirit. Cast them out.

Chronic Intractable Pain

On a Christian television program, a woman who had a morphine pump implant testified that she was healed of her chronic intractable pain and no longer required the medication from the pump.

Chronic Obstructive Pulmonary Disease (C.O.P.D.)

To a man with this condition: "I curse the cells, roots, and seeds and cast out the spirit of infirmity and rebuke this condition. I command a creative miracle with new lungs including bronchi and alveoli." He didn't need his oxygen.

Chronic Pancreatitis

"I command the pain to come out; I curse the inflammation to leave and a creative miracle with a new pancreas."

Colitis

"I curse the demonic spirit of infirmity and command it to come out. I command new tissues and a supernatural immunological system. Pain you come out in the name of Jesus." The woman I was praying for was healed.

Coma

People in coma can hear what is said so they can receive

the prayer of salvation. Their spirit and soul is still within.

Congenital Malformations

There is a startling and well documented testimony of a child with over twenty congenital abnormalities who was totally and instantly healed as reported by minister Bob Jones.

Creative Miracles

Such healings have been well documented. Carole Miller McCleery in her book, *Healings and Miracles*, experienced the regrowth of her amputated leg. I have personally witnessed replacement with new hips and knees after prayer. After a Charles and Frances Hunter meeting, a 12-year-old watched his neighbor's finger grow out along with a new fingernail just by commanding "grow." Benny Hinn described witnessing a man's leg regrow.

Crepitus

"I command the 'noise' in a damaged joint to come out, any pain to leave, and a creative miracle with new joints and tissues."

Crohns Disease

A Jewish medical colleague was treated by Dr. Crohn, but only Jesus can heal this—providing the person is open to Him and the Word.

Cystic Fibrosis

"I curse this spirit and command a creative miracle with new lungs, exocrine glands, and a supernatural immunological system."

Crepitus

"I command the 'noise' in a damaged joint to come out, any pain to leave, and a creative miracle with new joints and tissues."

Cystitis, Urinary Tract Infection

"I command the spirit of infection to come out and all of the lying urinary tract symptoms and signs to leave."

Deliverance Power

Check out a powerful prayer by Bob Bassler at www.jesussettingfree.com or call 1-574-234-8881 for deliverance.

Demonic Activity

British evangelist Smith Wigglesworth was awakened from a deep sleep by a sudden noise and saw Satan standing next to his bed. He said, "Oh, it's only you," and went back to sleep!

Demonic Book, Deliverance

Benny Hinn described a woman on the platform at one of

his meetings who was receiving a new lung. A word of knowledge revealed a demonic book she read had to be burned because it made her house unsafe.

Demonic Spirits

A woman and her husband were sitting in bed when he confessed about his unfaithfulness and she saw two demonic spirits enter into his body. A Christian artist saw multiple demonic spirits sitting throughout the pews as he entered his church.

Diabetes Mellitus

"I curse this and command a creative miracle with a new pancreas and the blood sugars to range at normal levels." When healed, check out the need for further medication.

Diagnosis, Unavailable

When no diagnosis is forth coming, you can assume the cause is probably demonic.

Disability

The goal is to eliminate the need for disabled parking spaces!

Dislocated Hip, Chronic

A pastor who was limping in a store, allowed me to place my hands on his hips and command the pain to go and for a creative miracle with new tissues. He was able to discard his cane without further limping.

Doctor Healed

Before Frances Hunter saw her surgeon I told her, '"Ask him, "How do you feel?"'rather than, '"How are you?"' As a result, she was able to minister to remove his neck pain and lead him to the Lord.

Dyslexia

"I command the spirit of infirmity to leave and I rebuke it and for normal speech to return." The man who received this prayer was surprised when he was healed.

Dysphagia

"I curse the source of this impairment and pain to leave with normal swallowing for both fluids and solids."

Ears

"I command the spirit of deafness to come out with a creative miracle for new hearing components including restoration of the organ of Corti and normal hearing."

Eating and Prayer

I asked a little girl if they prayed before they ate. She told me, "No, we don't have to. My mom's a good cook!"

Praying before you eat is wisdom. (Say Exodus 23:25)

Elbow Contracture with Pain

"I curse the spirit of infirmity and trauma and command the contracture to leave and the elbow to return to normal function with a full range of motion."

Endometriosis

"I rebuke the spirit of endometriosis and cast it out and the spirit of infirmity and for all pain to go in the name of Jesus." The woman I prayed for had no further abdominal pain.

Eyes, Absence

Pastor David Hogan initially didn't notice there were no eyes or orbits on the face of this newborn. The mother handed her baby to him and after he ministered, the child was totally normal.

Eye Glasses

During a healing service, pastor Tim Storey walked over and removed a person's glasses from their face and said, "You won't need these anymore." And, thank God, they didn't.

Fear, Spirit of

Fear is Satan's favorite weapon because it is so

destructive. Memorize the spiritual weapon against fear: *"For God has not given us a spirit of fear, but of power and of love and of a sound mind"* (2 Tim.1:7). Fear-based responses can produce chemical changes and cause damage to the body.

Fibrocystic Disease of the Breast

To a woman with this disease I prayed, "I command these lesions to dry up and leave her body and a creative miracle with new breast tissue." She agreed she was healed without checking. When she did, her lumps had vanished.

Fibromyalgia

"I command this spirit to come out." I touched the woman's forehead and instantly her pain resolved. Her nonrestorative sleep pattern also returned to normal.

Floaters

These minute black specks that float in the field of vision are called *mouches volantes*, meaning little "cobwebs." I commanded them to come out of a person and they did.

Foot Drop, Unrelieved by Surgery

I prayed for a man with this condition, "I command the fibrosis, adhesions, and scarring to come out of all tissue and for the nerves to be totally restored with normal strength and sensation." He was healed.

Foreign Countries *(testimonies from)*

Africa: Enlarged Heart

I commanded a creative miracle with a new heart for a woman with postpartum cardiomegaly and it was smaller on X-ray after prayer.

Australia: Arthritis

I prayed for a woman with this condition and her spirit of arthritis came out following a prayer for unforgiveness. Her pain resolved.

Germany: Bronchitis, Hearing Impairment

I prayed these words over a woman who had difficulty hearing: "I command the spirit of deafness to leave and the spirit of infection to come out and for a creative miracle with new lungs." Both her hearing and her bronchitis were restored.

India: Spinal Muscular Atrophy

I ministered to the parents of a 14-month-old who received movement in her extremities, even though it was minimal. I encouraged them to keep thanking Jesus on a daily basis.

Kenya: Tuberculosis

For a minister: "I command the spirit of infection to come out and a creative miracle with new lungs." I had him take two deep breaths and blow them out because I believe demonic spirits leave with this maneuver.

Nigeria: Stomach Cancer

"I command this foul spirit of cancer to come out." I received frequent telephone calls confirming this minister's complete healing.

Gall Bladder with Stones

For a women who was about to undergo an operation: "I command all the gall stones to be dissolved and come out in the name of Jesus." Her surgery was cancelled.

Gangrene of Foot

I received a call from a man in Los Angeles who was scheduled for an amputation from trauma suffered in a motorcycle accident. The note he wrote read: "My foot was healed right before my own eyes! I turned my blind faith over to my Savior Jesus Christ who has always been blessing me and continues to do so every single day. With Jesus, anything is possible."

Glaucoma

"I curse any damage to the eye and optic nerve and

command a creative miracle with normal pressure, normal flow, normal drainage of blood and fluid, and 20/20 vision." I stress the importance and necessity for everyone to call back to their doctor for a follow-up, for they may require a second dose of healing, especially when the devil attempts to steal the Word.

Gout

To a woman with this condition, "I command the spirit of gout to leave, the pain, the swelling and erythema (redness) to go, with normal metabolism and normal uric acid levels." She became asymptomatic.

Hand, Pain

During prayer at a Full Gospel Business Men's Fellowship International meeting, I held only a portion of a man's hand. He said, "God told me my hand would be healed today and you were holding the fourth and fifth fingers where I use to have severe pain."

Harrington Rods, for Back Pain

Charles Hunter saw a man healed of pain. He was able to bend over and touch his toes; normally impossible.

Headaches

There are numerous causes and usually there is relief when you command the headaches and source of the pain to go. A minister was healed of a ruptured aneurysm. A girl's headache resolved while just talking to her. Get medical help if the condition persists.

Hearing "Pops Open"

After ministering to a woman, I spoke into her ear, "Pa, Pa, Pa," and suddenly, her hearing "popped open" and she could hear.

Heart Disease, Congestive Heart Failure

"I command a creative miracle with a new heart," I said, praying for a man's heart condition. Later he told me his doctor was surprised his heart had not sounded so good in 15 years. He told the physician he saw another doctor. "Who was it, if I might ask?" The patient replied, "Dr. Jesus."

Hell

The greatest tragedy ever is not dying from a cancer, but from the permanent torment after being cast into hell for all eternity in your spiritual body.

Hematuria

A man came for prayer with this condition. I commanded the hematuria and whatever its source to cease and desist and commanded a creative miracle with a new bladder and kidneys. He knew he was healed.

Hepatitis

"I command the spirit of infection and all inflammation to come out and I command a creative miracle with a new liver."

Hernia, Umbilical

"I curse this hernia and command a creative miracle with the tissues to close in layers and for the hernia to leave in Jesus' name."

Hiccups

"I command the spirit of infirmity to come out and rebuke it. I command the spirit of hiccups to leave in the name of Jesus."

Hip Pain, Chronic

"I curse the damages to the hip to come out with a creative miracle and a new hip, pain to leave, and a full range of motion, and full weight bearing."

HIV

A woman with HIV was asked why she was healed. She answered because of my faith, continuously reading the Bible, repeating Scriptures, listening to tapes, and always carrying a prayer cloth.

HIV, Liver Cancer, Diabetes

I ministered the seven fundamental biblical revelations very carefully for this man who was a deteriorating picture of "skin and bones." His pain and swelling in the liver area resolved and I prayed for his HIV to leave as well. Several days later he started eating and reported his blood sugars were under a range of 100 mg.

Hydrocephalus

I ministered to an 18-month-old with obvious mental impairment anticipating a permanent feeding tube. The child stared into my eyes and mine into his as I spoke the Word to him in a spirit-to-spirit encounter. A doctor's report two weeks later revealed his head returned to normal size and he was now eating.

Hypertension

"I curse the elevated blood pressure and command a creative miracle with three distinct layers or tunics of new blood vessels with a normal pressure of 120/70."

Hypnosis

Cast out any demonic spirits which can enter anyone as the result of accepting hypnosis.

Hypothyroidism

"I command the spirit of infirmity to come out and curse

this thyroid disease with return of normal thyroid function."

Insomnia

"I command the spirit of fear, doubt, stress, strife, anxiety, grief, worry, and depression to come out. I speak the spirit of joy, love, and truth to go into them and especially the spirit of peace. I command all conflicts to come out and the spirit of sweet sleep when they go to bed."

Irritable Bowel Syndrome (I.B.S.)

"I command any impairment with bowels or other lying symptoms or signs to leave. I command a creative miracle with new bowels without further pain."

Knees, Degenerative Changes

"I curse the spirit of infirmity and arthritis and command a creative miracle with all new tissues"

Laryngitis

"I command the spirit of laryngitis to come out and rebuke it. I command the spirit of infection to go and command a creative miracle for new vocal cords and for the voice to return to normal."

Leprosy

Pastor David Hogan ministered to a man in an advanced

stage of leprosy and commanded "I break that power and render it powerless and ineffective." He reports that the man's deformed and disfigured body and skin was instantly replaced and healed.

Low Back Pain

For a man working in sales, I prayed, "I command pain to come out, muscles relax, full range of motion, and full weight bearing." The man couldn't believe his healing as he stood outside my home with my hand on his back.

Lupus Erythematous

I prayed for a woman with lupus: "I command the spirit of infirmity to come out along with all lying symptoms and lying signs." She was healed instantly.

Macular Degeneration

A woman finally agreed that because Jesus took this condition to the cross, she no longer had it. By His stripes she was healed. She told me, "My vision is crystal clear."

Microadenoma

I prayed for a man with this illness: "I command this spirit of infirmity to leave and I rebuke it and command this brain tumor to come out now and loose you in the name of Jesus." He had tears in his eyes and joy in his face.

Migraine

"I command this spirit of migraine to leave and any and all headache pain to clear and leave without any further recurrences."

Miracles, Signs, and Wonders

Andrew Wommack spoke resurrection life through faith that his youngest son Peter did not die because "The first report is not the last report." His son rose one hour and fifteen minutes later.

Evangelist R. W. Shambach visited a girl's sister in a foreign prison basically in solitary confinement. He blessed a candy bar which he was able to get to her through a guard. Shortly thereafter she was released and healed from her mental condition.

Mitral Valve Prolapse

Praying for a woman with this condition: "I curse the cells, roots, and seeds and command a creative miracle with a new heart and a normal mitral valve." In her "knower" she knew she was healed.

Multiple Sclerosis

I prayed for a woman with MS: "I command you spirit of infirmity to come out and I rebuke you. I command a creative miracle with a new brain and a new nervous system and for myelination to return to normal." Her parathesias and strength returned to normal.

Murder, Spirit of (Abortion)

After studying Psalm 139, 13-16, I have quoted this to pregnant women who are considering abortion: "*Before I formed you in the womb I knew [and] approved of you [as My chosen instrument], and before you were born I separated and set you apart, consecrating you; [and] I appointed you as a prophet to the nations*" (Jeremiah 1:5.) The four dimensional scanners reveal their "alive" babies. There can never be abortion control as long as sex is recreational. The next best thing is for them to consider adoption.

Muscular Dystrophy

I prayed for a girl with MD: "I command the spirit of infirmity to come out and I rebuke it. I command a creative miracle with all her muscles to return to normal strength and length and be healed in the name of Jesus." She was able to step up on a chair with great strength.

Neck Pain

Many times I have prayed, "I command the pain to leave, the muscles to relax, and for a full range of motion of the neck." The pain left these individuals.

Neurofibromatosis, Type One

"I curse the spirit of inheritance and generational curse to be reversed and nerve tissue tumors to go." I prayed this for a man who had multiple surgeries (as did his father) because of constant regrowth of these tissues. After ministering, he could run on the soles of his feet without pain.

Osteoarthritis

"I command the spirit of infirmity and arthritis to come out with normal bone. I command a creative miracle with all new tissues and for a full range of motion of the joints without pain."

Otitis Media

To a child with this ear problem: "I curse the cells, roots, and seeds, and any drainage and for the spirit of infection to come out." His mother reported the ear canals became totally clear.

Pacemaker

This documented miracle by Jesus through Kathryn Kuhlman involved both the disappearance of the cardiac pacemaker and the surgical scar. Dr. Richard Casdorph confirmed this healing through her ministry in his book.

Panic Attacks

"I command the strongman of the spirit of deaf and dumb to be cast out and expelled in the name of Jesus. I command total recovery without further panic attacks, anxiety, physiological appearing activities, or somatic, or cognitive lying symptoms."

Parkinson's Disease

"I command all lying symptoms and lying signs of Parkinson's disease be gone. I curse cogwheel rigidity demonstrated by flexing and extending the wrist, fenestrating gait with its quick, shuffling walking pattern, and tremor of his hands."

Partial Seizures

"I curse any focus in the brain and command the spirit of infirmity to come out without further activity. I command a miracle with a new brain." Inform all medications before taking them that "Jesus is my healer and either God or my doctor will stop it."

Peripheral Neuropathy

"I command these parathesias to come out without any further numbness. I curse the cells, roots, and seeds whatever the source of this condition with total recovery in the name of Jesus."

Pheblitis, Leg

"I curse any blockage or tissue damage to the vessels and command the spirit of infection to come out, pain to go, swelling to leave, and a creative miracle with return of normal circulation."

Plantar Wart

To a person with this condition: "I curse this lesion and command it to leave." It did.

Playing Vampire

A young boy took his Halloween custom very seriously and began to play vampire on a daily basis. Norvel Hayes told the boy's father his son needed deliverance, but the man refused to accept prayer for him. The boy deteriorated mentally and physically as he took on the character he was playing. When the father finally agreed to bring him for deliverance, the spirits knew what was planned and the child died that same morning.

Pneumonia

"I command the spirit of infection to come out with a creative miracle with new lungs and to be discharged tomorrow." The 6-year-old left the following morning.

Polycythemia Vera

"I command all the excessive RBC's (red blood cells) to leave and the bone marrow to be normal and produce the normal amount of RBC's."

Post Concussion Syndrome

"I command the spirit of infirmity to come out and I curse the cells, roots, and seeds of any damage to the brain and brain stem and command it to come out with total recovery."

Post Traumatic Arthritis

"I command pain from damp weather to come out and this spirit of arthritis to leave with a creative miracle with new tissues."

Poison

Lester Sumrall required help to preach at a healing service because he was poisoned from eating fish and became temporarily blind and incapacitated. Afterwards, the local pastor wanted him to lay hands on the sick but Lester really didn't have the strength. After ministering to the first person, who was healed, Lester himself was instantly healed.

Polio

"I command the spirit of infirmity to come out and I rebuke you. I command the spirit of infection to leave. I command a creative miracle with a new spinal cord, total strength, and normal ambulation."

Prayer Cloth, Anointed

When the prayer cloth I sent was received in Africa, the man reported his depression resolved and he felt total peace. Further, he was offered a position for a new job the following day.

Pregnancy

When I minister to the baby in a mother's womb, I ask, "May I pray for your baby with my hands on your stomach?" Then I pray, "In the name of Jesus and by the power of the Holy Spirit, I take total authority and dominion as I dedicate this baby to the Lord Jesus Christ of Nazareth. I command normal growth and development of this baby and I cast out any spirits of infirmity, unclean spirits, generational curses, spirits of inheritances, or chromosome, or gene abnormalities. I rebuke any harm to this child or the mother. Within three hours after the mother arrives at the hospital, Lord, open the birth canal fully and anoint it with the oil of the Holy Spirit and guide the baby to slide out without any pain or complications. I command the delivery of a healthy normal spontaneous full term child with an Apgar of ten. I place a seal of healing and protection on this baby and the mother with the blood of Jesus."

Pregnancy, Barren Mother

Frances Hunter says, "Father, Your Word says that the womb of your children will never be barren, and that you cause the barren woman to be the joyful mother of many children. I ask You to place in this womb a beautiful baby, perfect, whole and delivered within one year from today, in the name of Jesus! I also speak the desired gender into existence in the name of Jesus."

Prostatic Cancer with Metastasis

"I command this foul spirit of cancer to come out and rebuke it and curse the cells, roots, and seeds of this cancer. Any spread of cancer cells you come out now. I command a creative miracle with a new prostate functioning normally and a supernatural immunological system. I command a creative miracle with a new bone marrow. He will speak only positive affirmations."

Radial Neuropathy

"I command the spirit of infirmity to leave and a creative miracle for a new radial nerve with full return of strength and full extension of the hand."

Raising the Dead

The New Testament records many instances of Jesus raising people from the dead. And He declared we would do *"greater things than these"* (John 14:12). A great cardiologist friend, Dr. Chauncey Crandall, has seen four of his patients come back to life. Evangelist Vinny Longo, at the site of an accident, spoke to the victim, "Blood, you congeal in the name of Jesus and you come back into your body." He instantly sat up. Also, in a well documented case, Nigerian Pastor Daniel Ekechukwu died in a motor vehicle accident, but his wife refused to accept his death or release him and claimed Hebrews 11:35 as reason for him to live. *"[Some] women received again their dead by a resurrection."* He was taken by coffin to a service conducted by Reinhard Bonnke and came back to life even after being embalmed.

Command the spirit of death to come out and the spirit of life to return to their body. Command the body to be resurrected with normal vital signs and all sources of impairment to be healed in the name of Jesus. "I loose life back into his heart and I command it to begin pumping again." God should honor this if the person is not born again, or they have not completed their work, of if God gives you the word to proceed.

Reflex Sympathetic Dystrophy *(Complex Regional Pain Syndrome)*

"I curse the cells, roots, and seeds of this chronic nerve damage and command the spirit of infirmity and pain to leave. I command a creative miracle with a new nervous system."

Renal Disease

"I curse the cells, roots, and seeds of this disorder, and command a creative miracle with healthy functioning nephrons and new kidneys." I prayed this for a woman and she needed no renal dialysis.

Rheumatoid Arthritis

"I command the spirit of infirmity to come out and curse the damage to his joints and command total healing with all new tissues."

Rotator Cuff

During a live television program, a woman phoned in for healing. She later came into the TV studio with her arms raised above her head because her right wrist had been secured to her waist with a belt for six months. She cancelled her scheduled surgery.

Sarcoidosis

To a woman with this condition: "I command this spirit of infirmity to come out and a creative miracle with new lungs." Her breathing immediately improved.

Scar

"I command the scarring, fibrosis, and adhesions to come out of the scar on her face and for a creative miracle with new baby skin to replace the scar." After praying this over a woman with facial scars, she thanked Jesus for her healing.

Schizophrenia, Mental Disorders

See the Deliverance Power at the beginning of this chapter. Healings have been reported by people who have slept with a Bible under their pillow.

Scoliosis

For one woman, I commanded a creative miracle with a new spine and for all the tissues to line up with the Word of God. I commanded a full range of motion of her spine. Her spine became straight.

Sexual Impurity

Sin is the only thing that can separate our soul from God. Sin is suicide. It's **S**elf **I**nflicted **N**onsense. A way to release demonic control is to give your body to God.

Sinusitis

"I command the spirit of infection to come out and for a creative miracle with new sinuses. I command any spirit of allergies to leave and for a supernatural immunological system." Before and after praying, tap your finger over each of the sinus areas and witness the absence of tenderness after the healing.

Sjogren's Syndrome

A woman had lack of tears with dryness in eyes, mouth, and lips, but I told her she was normal. I told her to speak what she wanted instead of what she had—and to be moved only by what she believed. She was to speak the truth in advance and from her spirit rather than her mind. This is true faith. I explained how Jesus took Sjogren's Syndrome (and every other illness) to the cross. I then ministered to her and she started crying with tears.

Sleep Apnea

"I command any obstruction to this airway to come out and I cancel further episodes of apnea."

Smoking

"I command the spirit of bondage to come out and the spirit of nicotine and muscarine to leave. I command the spirit of infirmity to leave and a creative miracle with new lungs." In most cases, even the odor of smoke disappears. I have them say continuously, "Thank you Jesus for delivering me from cigarette smoking and setting me free."

Spinal Cord Paralysis

The followers of Christ in the early church delivered and healed the people, and so can you, because God is no respecter of persons. *"For foul spirits came out of many who were possessed by them, screaming and shouting with a loud voice, and many who were suffering from palsy or were crippled were restored to health"* (Acts 8:7). This means you can command a creative miracle, including a new spinal cord.

Spinal Muscular Atrophy

I commanded the spirit of inheritance and generational curse to be reversed along with defective genes and the spirit of infirmity to come out of a 4-year-old. "I curse the cells, roots, and seeds of defective muscles and contractures, and command a creative miracle with new muscles and total return of strength." After ministering this several times over a few months, the child responded by moving her extremities.

Spinal Stenosis

"I command the spinal canal to open and release any pressure or swelling on the spinal nerve roots at their foramen or opening and all hypertrophic changes to go. I command fibrosis, adhesions, and, scarring, swelling and edema to come out. I command a Jesus Christ decompression and total return of previous normal function without pain or impairment."

Stomach, Ulcer

"I command the spirit of infection to come out and for a creative miracle with a new stomach and no further pain."

Stroke

To a woman who had suffered a stroke: "I command any dead cells to come out and the spirit of life to return to every cell of her brain as well as a creative miracle with a new brain. I command a creative miracle with a new nervous system and the strength to totally return to her extremities with normal walking." She praised the Lord and started running.

Stuttering

"I command this spirit of infirmity to leave and I rebuke this and command speech to return with a normal flow of words."

Temporal Arteritis

"I command the spirit of infirmity to come without any inflammation and for a creative miracle with new blood vessels."

Tenosynovitis

"I command the pain and the spirit of infirmity to leave and all lying symptoms and signs to go in the name of Jesus."

TMJ *(Temporomandibular Joint disorders)*

I prayed these words for a woman with this condition: "I curse the cells, roots, and seeds of any damage to the area and command a creative miracle for all new tissues and for them to line up and function physiologically in the perfection to which God created them." She had total recovery.

Thoracic Pain

A woman was suffering with this and I prayed: "I command the pain to come out now." The pain left and she said she could still feel the heat from my hand—even though I couldn't.

Throat, Foreign Body

I prayed for a women in an emergency room at the hospital. "I command the foreign body to come out. Several minutes later she vomited a piece of meat. The laryngoscopy procedure was cancelled and she was discharged from the ER.

Thumb, Chronic Dislocation

"I curse this dislocation in this minister and command a creative miracle with full range of motion of this thumb and no further restrictions."

Tinnitus

"I command you spirit of tinnitus to come out now."

Tongues

It is powerful and vital to pray in tongues, but after you minister healing since the devil can't understand it.

Trigiminal Neuralgia

"I command a creative miracle with a new fifth nerve and tissues with a spiritual Teflon sponge to cover and protect the nerve and for the pain to leave."

Tumor, Posterior Hard Palate

I cursed a tumor on a woman and commanded it to leave in the name of Jesus. As she received the anointing on her forehead she actually felt the tumor disappear.

Ulnar Nuropathy

"I curse any damage and command a creative miracle with a new ulnar nerve without any impairment." To test, press the tips of the thumb and fifth fingers tightly held together. Then determine if there is any weakness by attempting to pull the fingers apart with your finger inserted between them.

Upper Respiratory Infection—Flu, Cold

"I command the spirit of infection to come out and any lying symptoms or lying signs to leave in the name of Jesus."

Uterine Fibroids, Pregnant Woman

I prayed for a woman who had this condition and commanded the fibroids to come out and the spirit of infirmity and any pressure on the fetus from the uterus to leave. The baby was able to be carried and delivered full term without sequelae.

Varicose Veins

"I curse the abnormal veins and command a creative miracle with new veins and normal valves." I have seen women totally healed as a result of this prayer.

Vein of Galen Malformation

A pastor's son had a rare blood tumor in the back of his head. I had the privilege of leading his neurosurgeon to the Lord through the prayer of salvation. The preoperative procedure to reduce the blood flow with embolization was incomplete, yet a miracle occurred during the procedure with total recovery without sequelae.

Vitiligo

A woman with this disorder came for prayer. "I curse the cells, roots, and seeds and command all the depigmentation to be totally filled in and replaced with normal pigmentation. I commanded the melanocytes to return to normal." Three months later there was almost total recovery in her face.

Vision

John Osteen (the father of pastor Joel Osteen) once had

a vision of the devil yelling at him. He called for Jesus, who showed up standing in front of him. He asked for Jesus' help again since he could still hear the hollering. With that, the Lord took a step back into John's body and he became one in Christ. John learned the secret of having peace.

Worry and Fear, Demon of

A minister visiting a church saw a demonic spirit of fear attach itself to a woman's neck. He boldly told the spirit of fear to leave and she was totally delivered.

Zoster, Herpes (Shingles)

"I command this pain to come out now and the skin lesions to go and the blessings of a supernatural immunological system."

A Final Word

My prayer for you is that what you have read on these pages will become much more than just information and interesting accounts of stories being *taught* to you. God has prepared you to be used beyond your greatest spiritual imagination in miraculous ways during these end times—for this boldness has been *caught* by you as you lay hands on those who need healing and/or deliverance and see them recover.

– Phillip Goldfedder, M.D.

For Additional Resources or to Schedule the Author for Speaking Engagements, Contact:

Rev. Phillip Goldfedder, M.D.
5 Cathy Circle
Warrenville, SC 29851

Neurosurgeon

Alternative Medicine Healing Ministry, Inc.
Phone: (Office) 803-644-4854
(Cell) 803-640-3507
Fax: 803-643-1096

Websites: www.healingisyours.com
www.healingcenterofcsra.com

Email: 7777777JC@BELLSOUTH.NET